# BLESSED TO BLESS

by Randy Blackaby

ONESTONE
BIBLICAL RESOURCES

Published by:
One Stone Press
979 Lovers Lane
Bowling Green, KY 42103


Printed in the United States of America

ISBN 10: 0-98549-388-7
ISBN 13:  978-0-9854938-8-2

**Supplemental Materials Available:**

➢ Power Point Slides for each lesson

➢ Answer Key

➢ Downloadable PDF


www.onestone.com

**ONE STONE**

*BIBLICAL RESOURCES*

# Introduction

The staff at One Stone appreciates the opportunity to bring this material to you. It has been our pleasure and honor to work with Karen Blackaby, fulfilling her desire to publish her husband's work after his unexpected death in 2011. Randy was a newspaper reporter and editor, gospel preacher, elder, and publisher of articles and workbooks. He was well qualified to produce this much needed material for study today.

The effects of materialism are destructive to the most precious things we possess: our relationship with others, with our families, with the church, and with God. So many people are trading their eternal reward for the temporary pleasures of earthly possessions. As a diligent Bible student and gifted writer, Randy addressed this need.

In working with Randy Blackaby's material to prepare it for printing, I had the opportunity to study his material. After the introductory lesson on the need for this study, Randy gives an overview of the Old Testament and the teachings of Jesus regarding material blessings and possessions. God's material blessings and the role they play in the relationship with the people of Old, help one develop a better perspective of their possessions today.

Beginning with lesson 7 and continuing through lesson 10, Randy discusses some practical topics relating specifically to today. Considering the growing problems with materialism, debt, and bankruptcy, it is apparent these topics need to be discussed in more detail, with scripture, and application.

The remaining lessons discuss giving within the concepts of being like God. He is the author of giving and has blessed us abundantly. As recipients, we need to be faithful stewards of God's blessings.

This material is recommended for adult Bible studies, small group and in home studies, and for teens (high school age & above). This is valuable material for equipping teens to be prepared for the important decisions they will face in marriage, careers, and using their possessions. There have been some minor revisions in the editing process, however, Randy wrote the material. The additions to this material relate to the questions at the end of the lessons.

On behalf of the staff at One Stone, we hope you enjoy this material and find it profitable.

# Foreword

I moved to the Dayton, Ohio area in January, 2011. Randy Blackaby was preaching in nearby New Carlisle. He reached out to me and we quickly formed a friendship. We spoke of a number of things as our friendship grew, including this workbook.

Randy had seen the need for Biblical instruction on the subject of money. He had watched several Christians make terrible financial decisions over the years: some of them getting into trouble with their credit cards, others repeating foolish choices and living beyond their means, and still others attempting to walk away from their debts by filing for bankruptcy. In a day when the churches of men are hosting financial seminars for their members, Randy knew that preachers, elders, and Bible Class teachers should be able to simply open the Bible and give brethren needed instruction regarding their finances.

At the time Randy and I had met, this material had already been used by his son Joshua in a Bible class at the Douglass Hills church of Christ in Louisville, KY. However, Randy told me the material still needed to be "polished up" before he would submit it for publication. Like many of us, this was something he intended to "get around to doing," but he had more pressing issues on his plate at the time.

Randy passed away unexpectedly on Thursday, January 3, 2013. Despite the suddenness of Randy's passing, his wife Karen moved quickly to see that this material was published. I am grateful for her decision. "This," she said, "is something I can do for him." Two of their sons, Joshua and Ezra, gave me copies of the files containing the material for this workbook. I passed these files on to the folks at One Stone, and they finished the work Randy was not able to "get around to doing."

Randy Blackaby was a diligent Bible student and a gifted writer. I believe the material you have before you is the best that can be found in our brotherhood on this subject. May you use it to God's glory.

Heath Rogers
Beavercreek, OH
October 10, 2013

# TABLE OF CONTENTS

# WHY THIS STUDY IS NEEDED

Do we really need a workbook on what the Bible says about money, finances and possessions? To help answer this question, consider some of the following:

- According to the National Council on Problem Gambling, 85% of U.S. adults have gambled at least once in their lifetimes, 60% in any given year (Morrison, 2013).

- Millions of Americans file for bankruptcy each year, including a fair number of Christians. Misuse of debt and greedy materialism cause many of these bankruptcies.

- According to a New York Times article by Ron Lieber, the risk that any marriage will end in divorce is 45% (Lieber, 2013). Financial conflicts are a leading cause of these divorces.

- Many recognize financial worries is a contributing factor to the growing problem of sleep disorders.

While it is impossible to accurately document what Christians give in their Lord's Day offerings, Internal Revenue Service analysis shows, if the Americans who itemize their deductions, the average American gives less than three percent to church and charity combined. Polling done among professed Christians by The Barna Group confirms this. They find giving to churches amounts to about 2.2 percent of income ("American Donor Trends," 2013).

If such numbers also reflect the giving patterns of members of the Lord's church, then clearly brethren need more study and instruction concerning proportionate giving. Brethen should fulfill the commands to "lay something aside, storing up as he may prosper," and to do so "bountifully" and with "all liberality" (1 Cor. 16:1-2; 2 Cor. 8:6, 11).

> ...The average American **gives less** than **three percent** to church and charity combined.

# Money
## is not something that can be **ignored.**

"Psychologists tell us that people think about money more than they do about sex," says Gary Moore (Moore, 2003). This is not surprising. There is a power in money and possessions. In fact, it can have the power of life and death. With it, we can buy life-essentials like food, clothing, and shelter. We can give money or possessions to save the starving, the unclothed, and the unsheltered.

An abundance of material wealth gives us freedoms not enjoyed without it. With money, we are better able to do as we please— travel, be entertained, educated, and enjoy good things.

Without money or possessions, life can be miserable. At best, the poor face mere subsistence. Lack of such resources often results in unhealthy squalor or death.

Money is not something that can be ignored. "Money matters. It seems that money, like sex, is at the core of everything that we human beings do. The life-giving power of money in modern society is god-like," writes J. Schreider (Banks & Stevens, 1997). Herein is the temptation, to see money as the real power rather than God, who is the original source of every good thing in our world.

Jacques Ellul has written that life is full of paradox and ambiguity so that money can become a god, "Mammon," or merely a medium of exchange (Ellul, 2004). Wealth can be associated with either the curses or the blessings of God's law. The key, he suggested, is letting God lead us through these difficulties, puzzles, and tensions.

Money can be a good servant to the righteous, but it also can become a master, as Jesus suggested in Matthew 6:24. Money requires someone strong enough to control it. It appears most people are ruled by money most of the week, leaving just a small amount of time for the Lord on Sunday.

This compartmentalization of faith produces a morally split personality, or a Sunday versus Monday outlook on faith and life. Many Christians are very uncomfortable when money and possessions are discussed in the context of a Bible class or a sermon.

Men as diverse as Thomas Jefferson and Karl Marx were critical of religion, in part because they saw religion ignoring poverty and just trying to look beyond it. However, the Bible declares, "Pure and undefiled religion before God and the Father is this: to visit orphans and widows in their trouble, and to keep oneself unspotted from the world" (James 1:27).

## We Need A Biblical Perspective Of Money, Finances

We cannot separate our spiritual lives from our money, how we use it, and what we think about it. Failing to understand this relationship has resulted in a failure to really see how the latter reflects the actual nature of the former.

It is not unusual for members of the church to do an exhaustive study of all the Bible says about faith, baptism, or marriage, divorce and remarriage. We comprehensively review all Jesus, the apostles, and other New Testament writers say about salvation, holiness and morality. There seems to be a dearth of effort to explore all that the Bible says about material possessions.

Members of the church hold a number of disparate views about the proper place of money and possessions in the life of a Christian. Many view material things as totally temporal or earthly, having no spiritual quality. Some of our views are overly simple, focusing only on one aspect of what Scripture teaches about money and possessions. It is easy to ignore Scriptures not fitting our perspective on money and then highlight others supporting our point of view.

## False Or Limited Views About Material Things

1. God wants every Christian to be wealthy. This is the health and wealth doctrine popularized by some TV evangelists like Jim Bakker, Oral Roberts, Benny Hinn and Kenneth and Gloria Copeland. It is a Disneyland gospel where the good guys all get rich. Being wealthy equates to spirituality. Taken to its logical conclusion, if a person is poor or only of moderate means, he or she must be spiritually weak or sinful. It "syncretizes Christianity with selfish individualism and the materialism of our age" (Moore, 2003).

2. All wealth is evil. This takes the opposite view of the first. Those holding this view assume if anyone is wealthy, they became so through sinful conduct and the exploitation of others. This approach assumes those who are rich are materialistic and those who are poor aren't. In this view, poverty is a virtue. A bare subsistence living is all this view allows.

3. A Christian should totally depend upon God for all provisions. If a person makes an effort to advance his own wellbeing or prosperity, he is showing a lack of faith in God. This view does not allow a person to plan for the future. When any reversal of the normal occurs, others must aid these persons financially. Perhaps most importantly, proponents of this view essentially see "receiving" as more spiritual than "giving," a view lacking in scriptural support. It is interesting to speculate about who would do the giving if everyone adopted this approach.

4. Material things and spiritual things are totally independent of one another. There is physical life with its material issues, and there is spiritual life in a entirely different realm of thought and behavior.

## Four Possible Reactions

1. Some simply reject as much of life in the material realm as is possible. Monks, monasteries, and some of the more recent communal movements (Hippies of 1960s, for

example—RB), reflect this direction. Whether the goal is an escape from the sinful world or just "dropping out," it contradicts biblical directives to be diligent and work honorably (1 Cor. 10:31; Eph. 6:5-7; Col. 3:22-24).

2. The opposite reaction is total immersion in the material world, focusing solely on the acquisition of money and possessions. This lifestyle results in total identification with "this world," in the sense described in 1 John 2:15-17. Jesus declared men and women can live in the world without being a part of the world (John 17:15-19).

3. The third and popular reaction splits one's life into two spheres, follows the Bible in what is viewed as the spiritual half of life, and uses a worldly "business model" in the realm of economics. One writer calles this approach "spiritual schizophrenia."

4. The final reaction and the one this author views as scriptural is involvement in whatever economic system we find ourselves, using biblical principles to provide for ourselves and accomplish God's other purposes in our lives.

### Issues To Be Resolved

- Are material things God's provision for His creation or a temptation to evil and sin?

- Is money good, evil, or neutral?

- Does God want us totally and immediately dependent upon Him for everything, or does he want us to assume at least partial responsibility for our own material welfare?

- Does the Bible teach anything about how men are to acquire wealth?

- What do the Scriptures say, if anything, about producing and owning material things?

- Is there any connection between how we use our finances and our spiritual maturity?

### Money A Common Subject In Bible

The Bible says more about money than heaven and hell combined. There is something about material wealth and poverty in every major segment of the Bible from Genesis to Revelation. One writer's research shows 2,350 verses in the Bible dealing with money. This is about twice as many as there are on faith and prayer combined. The only subject Jesus spoke more about money is the kingdom of God itself (Alcorn, 2001).

Another writer says, "If we were to strike the comments of Jesus about money, we would reduce his teachings by more than one-third. Sixteen of Jesus' approximately 38 parables dealt with money. One of every seven verses in the first three gospels in some way deals with money" (Grimm, 1992).

Of all of Jesus' teachings, His statements about money have been the most perplexing to those who first heard Him and those who read His words today. The Lord's teaching almost always leaves us thinking, examining ourselves and, sometimes, feeling guilty.

Certainly, Christians ought to be able to agree that we need to learn how to keep our hearts free from the love of money, which God's Word identifies as the "root" of all sorts of evil (1 Tim. 6:10). Any teaching about work, stealing, bribery or covetousness necessarily involves a discussion of money and possessions. We hardly can discuss the biblical directive to "not love the world or the things of the world" (1 John 2:15-17) without concretely dealing with the world's measuring cup (money).

Often ignored in church Bible studies, and sidetracked as issues of mere personal judgment, are matters of wisdom in the use of God's material blessings. The Old Testament book of Proverbs is full of guidance in this regard and the New Testament elaborates and expands upon that wisdom.

Many Christians ignore biblical principles regarding how they are to use money. Instead, they imagine supporting a particular economic or political system will solve issues of distribution and use of their financial resources. However, no economic or political system eliminates covetousness, creates sympathy for the needy, eliminates hoarding and waste, or assures money gained will not be used to exert ungodly power over others. Often almost totally overlooked is the fact that the Bible positively tells us how to make money and how to use our money, not just how not to misuse it.

### The Bottom Line

Fearing God is more valuable than money or possessions. A person does not always have to make a choice between the two. However, when a choice is demanded, the words of Proverbs 15:16 seem crucial: "Better is a little with the fear of the Lord, than great treasure with trouble."

Understanding the proverbs to be "general truths," not unqualified promises, we also observe that God provides riches, honor and a good life to those who are humble and fear God (Prov. 22:4). There are temporary exceptions to these general truths, as the life of Job illustrates, though the blessings of God always accrue to the faithful in the final accounting.

The New Testament does not appear to link directly physical blessings to faithfulness as the Old Testament does. The latter may well serve as a physical pattern of the spiritual blessings available through faithfulness in Christ.

### Issues About Money And Possessions

The relation between our material things and Christian faith has been an issue of debate and disagreement for centuries. Should Christians have possessions? If so, how much should they have? Can a person have too much? Different people professing to be Christians have answered these questions differently, the extremes reflected in the asceticism of the monks and the luxury of those who preach a health and wealth gospel.

Sometimes these divergent approaches are attributed to what is perceived as two different voices of Scripture on money. One voice tells us material things are to be received as a blessing from God. The other voice warns us money and materialism is a curse and the rich are hardly able to enter the kingdom of God. These two voices are a reality in Scripture. Christians must determine whether both can be understood as a harmonious message from God.

The general rule of the Old Testament message is when men are faithful to God they prosper. This is illustrated in examples like Job, Abraham, Jacob, Joseph and others. This principle is a major element of the wisdom literature, particularly the Proverbs. The book of Job illustrates there can be and are exceptions to the general rule.

The New Testament presents Jesus as poor, often homeless, and dependent upon the love of others for provision at times. It presents wealth as one of the most serious temptations and impediments to entering the Kingdom of Heaven. As noted above, the New Testament describes the "love of money" as "a root of all kinds of evil."

Are these two views opposed or are they to be harmonized? Did God's view and use of material possessions change as the old covenant was "nailed to the cross" (Col. 2:14) or is the teaching of the New Testament corrective elaboration and fuller revelation of God's intent for man's use of the material?

Unless we are able to reach some conclusions on these issues, we'll be unable to form a comprehensive view of God's teachings on money and possessions. Guilty feelings, confusion, and sin are three potential results of not understanding God's will in this area of our lives.

It is hoped each student sees the critical need for this study. The Apostle Paul's admonition to "Be diligent (study-KJV) to present yourself approved to God, a worker who does not need to be ashamed, rightly dividing the word of truth" (2 Tim. 2:15) is as important here as when exploring other issues.

## Cited

Morrison, William. (2013, October 10). *Gambling statistics*. Retrieved from http://www.myaddiction.com/education/articles/gambling_statistics.html.

Lieber, R. (2009, October 23). *Money talks to have before marriage*. Retrieved from http://www.nytimes.com/2009/10/24/your-money/24money.html?_r=0.

*American donor trends*. (2013, April 12). Retrieved from https://www.barna-update/culture/606-american-donor-trends.

Moore, G. (2003). *Faithful finances 101*. (p. 39). Philadelphia and London: Templeton Foundation Press.

Banks, R., & Stevens, R. P. (1997). *The complete book of everyday christianity*. (pp. 658-663). Downers Grove, IL: Intervarsity Press.

Ellul, J. (2004). Money and power. Downers Grove, IL: Intervarsity Press.

Moore, G. (2003). *Faithful finances 101*. (p. 12). Philadelphia and London: Templeton Foundation Press.

Alcorn, R. (2001). The treasure principle. (pp. 3-4). Colorado Springs, CO: Multnomah Books.

Grimm, E. (1992). Generous people. (p. 19). Nashville, TN: Abingdon Press.

## ➢ Questions ◁

Be sure to do your homework because what you discover will become part of our study and discussion during class.

1. What is the most troublesome question about money, for Christians, in your opinion? _____
_____
_____

2. If money and possessions are "gifts" from God, why do they become such a source of temptation and sin? _____
_____
_____

3. Why do you think Christians are uncomfortable talking with one another about "money issues" in the context of faith, spirituality or the church? _____
_____
_____

4. What is it that determines whether money will become your "servant" or your "master"?_____
_____

5. In terms of achieving the highest level of spirituality, which is the better economic position?

   ■ Poverty

   ■ Moderate wealth

   ■ Considerable wealth

   Be ready to explain your answer in class. Give some supporting texts from the Bible. ___
   _____
   _____
   _____

6. Does one's view of what the Bible teaches about money help shape one's political views? _____ Explain your answer: _____
_____
_____

7. What would you like to learn from this study? _____
_____
_____
_____

# WHAT THE BIBLE FIRST TEACHES ABOUT MONEY

As we search for a biblical perspective on money and possessions, the logical place to start is the beginning. This means turning our attention to the first book of the Bible, the book of Genesis, the book of beginnings.

There is nothing in this material world money buys that God did not create in the beginning. He is the creator of all things (John 1:3). Man creates nothing materially. We merely take the raw materials of the original creation and modify and manage them. The Scriptures describe this as the "dominion" (rule or power) God granted man over all the creation (Gen. 1:26). This authority over the material creation is a stewardship, a delegated or subordinate dominion. God still owns all things (Psa. 24:1; 1 Cor. 10:26, 28).

As we explore money and possessions and the moral issues involved with both, it is worth observing as God created our world incrementally, He declared each portion to be "good" (Gen. 1:10, 12, 18, 21, 25, 31). In fact, verse 31 declares, "Then God saw everything that He had made, and indeed it was very good."

God placed Adam, His first human creation, in the Garden of Eden. The garden was pleasant to the eye, enjoyable, and a perfect material environment (Gen. 2:8-16). The Lord then created a sexual companion fully suited to Adam. Adam and Eve were naked, their sexuality and physical differences fully open—and they had no reason to be ashamed (Gen. 2:25).

We can thus conclude material things themselves are not evil as some human philosophies such as asceticism or monasticism have implied. Genesis also records the beginning of sin and its effects upon the human race, thus enabling us to see that man's sinful attitudes and behaviors are what transform material blessings into evil curses.

To a large degree, the rest of the Bible record demonstrates only through faith in God and His commandments can men success-fully use material things for their good and happiness. Sinfully

**...authority** over the material creation is a **stewardship**...

**God** still **owns all** things.

used, the very same material things become producers of all sorts of evil, shame, harm and unhappiness.

### Lessons From Abraham

Following man's fall into sin and God's cleansing and recreation of the world through the Flood of Noah's day, the Bible introduces a man of phenomenal faith Abraham to us. We almost instantly learn Abraham was wealthy, immensely blessed in this manner by God (Gen. 13:2, 6; 24:35).

We observe Abraham's obedience to God superceded his concerns about money and wealth. Called by God to leave his homeland, Abraham left his social position and economic security in Mesopotamia to go where God sent him (Gen. 12:1, 4-5).

Abraham did not let wealth or its potential accumulation cause division in his family. When he and Lot's flocks were too great for the land on which they dwelt, Abraham gave Lot first choice of where to dwell, even though tradition would have given the older man precedence.

Further, in God's promises to bless Abraham and his descendants (Gen. 12:1-3) was a direct pledge to give them "great possessions" (Gen. 15:14). This was accomplished first in the plunder Israel brought out of Egypt during the Exodus (Exod. 12:35-36) and more fully when God gave them the land of Canaan with all its houses, vineyards, livestock and other material goods for which they had not labored (Deut. 6:10-11; Josh. 24:13).

The student of the Old Testament observes material blessings were at the heart of the reward God promised Israel if they would be obedient. The reward of physical blessings to the patriarchs creates and develops a pattern for the spiritual rewards and heaven promised under the covenant of Christ.

Whether we are considering material or spiritual blessings, the Bible is clear. God gives them generously to those who are faithful to him. From Genesis forward, we learn God's blessings are intimately connected to obedience. This principle seen in the physical world and material blessings extends into the spiritual realm. It is a pattern still discernable in our physical lives, to one degree or another, teaching us also how to gain heaven, eternal life, and all else God promises Christians.

### The Example Of Joseph

Toward the end of the Genesis account, we find another dramatic example of how God lifts up and rewards the faithful. Joseph, one of the 12 sons of Jacob, sold into slavery in Egypt by his brothers, remained faithful under every temptation and trial.

> The **reward** of **physical** blessings to the patriarchs creates and develops a **pattern** for the **spiritual rewards** and heaven **promised** under the covenant of **Christ**.

As a result, God providentially raised him up to be the second highest ruler in the most powerful nation of his day. He became second only to Pharaoh in Egypt, which provided him access to great riches and power (Gen. 41:39-44).

This pattern is replicated again and again in the Old Testament history. During the captivity, Daniel is taken captive to Babylon. Because of his continued obedience and faithfulness, God elevated him to be governor over all Babylon in the days of Nebuchadnezzar (Dan. 2:48). Later, he rose to the third highest position in all of Babylon in the last days of Belshazzar (Dan. 5:29). Great wealth, in addition to power, accompanied these promotions. He ruled in the most powerful nation of his day.

The book of Esther records how a Jewish slave girl, faithful to God and her nation, risks her life to preserve her nation and God's conduit for blessing the entire world. She becomes the queen of Persia and thus is blessed with great wealth. She also influenced the most powerful nation of her day.

### Lessons From Exodus

The heart of the Exodus story reveals a faithful and loving God rescuing His people from slavery, misery, and poverty. In doing so, He gives them the riches of Egypt and promises of even greater unearned prosperity in the land of Canaan.

As in Genesis, it is clear all physical blessings ultimately find their source in God. Physical blessings and material possessions are intrinsically good. If they were not, God would not have used them as a blessing for obedience or a motivation to faithfulness.

A careless reading of Exodus can lead to an overly material view of God's action. It is important to see God had larger objectives in His bestowal of material blessings on Israel. These blessings were designed to go deeper than mere reward for faithful obedience. They were designed to show the peoples of the earth that Jehovah indeed is God (Exod. 6:7; 9:16).

Israel's experience serves as a type of what might be called "the second exodus," the rescue of men and women from the slavery and misery of sin. The spiritual antitype does not negate the truth in the type. God often has blessed faithful men with material blessings. Disobedience to God often miraculously or naturally resulted in the loss of possessions, health, and happiness.

This critical lesson involves drawing the necessary inference from the example. People attain spiritual blessings in the same manner physical blessings are legitimately received—by obedience to God's will.

### The Law of Moses on Money

The book of Genesis outlines general principles about God's provision of material things for mankind. It also reports the beginning of sin and the first results of sin. From Exodus to Deuteronomy we find recorded God's first steps in providing for man's redemption. Included in these books is direction for handling material blessings individually and within the covenant God made with Israel.

Exodus records God's rescue of Israel from physical and economic misery (slavery) in Egypt and His promise of a land "flowing with milk and honey" (Exod. 3:8,17). It was God, not Israel, who made the nation rich and powerful.

Since Israel represented God to the world, there was a special need for them to demonstrate God's love for the world through special care for those among them who lacked wealth and power, especially the poor, the widowed, and the orphaned. Help was directed in the form of sharing, giving, and forgiving debts. If the law of God had been faithfully executed in the physical realm, it would have been a perfect illustration by Israel of God's love for mankind. The law itself served as this prophetic illustration, even if it was not faithfully obeyed for very long at a time among God's people.

The Law of Moses provided Israel with a detailed code of behavior for every aspect of life, material and physical. The law delivered at Mount Sinai spoke extensively regarding the acquisition, use, and sharing of material blessings. No other law among men, prior to the cross of Jesus, so extensively defined proper use of money and possessions.

It is not an overstatement to say God's law defined and regulated a holy economic system designed to benefit all men who were a part of it. When Israel obeyed God's commands, the nation was a model for the world of living in harmony with God's economic order.

It is important to understand the purpose of law, in general, and the Law of Moses, in particular, before we explore what God told Israel. The Apostle Paul wrote, "What purpose then does the law serve? It was added because of transgressions, till the Seed should come to whom the promise was made; and it was appointed through angels by the hand of a mediator" (Gal. 3:19). He further stated the law guarded, kept, and tutored men until Christ and justification by faith should come (Gal. 3:23-24).

Even a quick reading of Exodus through Deuteronomy shows Israel was a stubborn, fickle, and often faithless people. The Law of Moses served to define acceptable behavior and correct sinful inclinations and actions. God had created a perfect world, materially, economically and spiritually. Sin spoiled that perfection. Mankind needed control in the face of sin's temptations.

Upon finally receiving the Promised Land in the second generation, after 40 years of wandering and death in the wilderness, Israel received the bountiful blessings and material prosperity God had promised. The sinful temptations of wealth quickly presented themselves. The need for the law, given beforehand, became obvious.

God reversed the exodus many years later in the history of Israel, through captivities in Assyria, Babylon, Persia, and elsewhere when the nation became unfaithful. Part of that unfaithfulness included failure to care for the weak and poor among the covenant people (Micah 2:1-5; Amos 4:1-3; 5:10-13). Also, a large part was attributable to the idolatry that credited voiceless, motionless creations of man for the blessings flowing from Jehovah.

### Principles Evident In The Ten Commandments

The Ten Commandments provide a skeletal outline or summary of the entire Law of Moses. The first four commandments define God's expectations of Israel in regard to Himself. At least one of those, the Sabbath law (Exod. 20:8-11), addressed a principle regarding money and material possessions. God told Israel to work six days to obtain needed physical things, but to do no work on the seventh day. It was holy—to be focused on worship and the spiritual aspects of life.

God demonstrated during the wilderness wandering He could and would provide sufficiently for His people in six days so work on the seventh was not necessary. This is most clearly seen in His provision of manna and the rules He affixed to its gathering (Exod. 16:4-5). Later, the same provision was made in six years so a Sabbath year could be observed (Lev. 25:18-21).

The remainder of the commandments broadly delineates how God demanded His people behave toward one another. At least three of these commandments involve rules for the use of one's material possessions and attitudes and behavior relative to other people's possessions.

1. "Honor your father and mother" (Exod. 20:12). As Jesus demonstrated centuries later, this commandment involved not just respect or obedience, but caring for aged, ill, or poor parents (Mark 7:9-13).

2. "You shall not steal" (Exod. 20:15). This law precluded taking what didn't belong to you. It defined at least a limited concept of personal property rights. Arguably, commandments six and seven (not to murder or commit adultery) prohibit stealing life and stealing another's spouse.

3. "You shall not covet your neighbor's house; you shall not covet your neighbor's wife, nor his male servant, nor his female servant, nor his ox, nor his donkey, nor anything that is your neighbor's" (Exod. 20:17). The last commandment is comprehensive, forbidding not only the taking of a neighbor's possessions (stealing), but also strongly desiring another's possessions. This law addressed the attitude of heart controlling behavior as well as the sin of greed.

### Other Principles Concerning Money, Possessions

Beyond the fundamental principles outlined in the Ten Commandments, the Mosaical Law outlined specific rules and regulations for dealing with money and possessions within the nation of Israel and the covenant God made with them. If one reads beyond the Ten Commandments, first recorded in Exodus 20 and then re-read 40 years later, as recorded in Deuteronomy 5, a wide array of laws on such issues is quickly seen.

Here is an overview of some of these laws:
• Limitations were placed on slavery (indentured servitude due to debts) among the Israelites (Exod. 21:1-11, 20-21, 26-27).
• Payment of financial judgments was required for damages done through negligence (Exod. 21:28-36; 22:6-8; Lev. 24:18-20).
• Punitive financial judgments were required for purposeful damages (Exod. 22:1-5).
• God's people were not to afflict widows, orphans or the poor; particularly by charging them interest on loans or requiring harmful collateral (Exod. 22:22-27; Lev. 25:35-46; Deut. 23:19-20; 24:6, 10-13, 17). (We will deal with the issue of loans, interest, etc. more in another lesson.) They were not to show negative partiality to a poor man or pervert justice for him in a dispute (Exod. 23:3, 6; Lev. 19:15).
• It was allowable to eat of a neighbor's vineyard or field if one was hungry, but not to harvest more than what was immediately needed for nourishment (Deut. 23:24-25).
• The firstborn and firstfruits of all things belonged to the Lord, demonstrating that all physical blessings were from God and belonged, ultimately, to him (Exod. 22:29-30).
• Bribery was condemned because it perverted justice, sinfully using money or material things as a power to get one's own way (Exod. 23:8).
• The working of men, beasts and land was regulated through the Sabbath regulations so that it didn't conflict with spiritual duties toward God or toward fellow men (Exod. 23:10-12; 31:13-17: Lev. 25:1-7).

- Debts were to be forgiven twice each century so that families did not lose completely their inheritance in the Promised Land (Lev. 25:8-34; Deut. 15:1-6).
- Freewill giving was the standard given for funding God's house of worship (Exod. 25:1-9: 35:4-9, 20-29).
- Corners of grain fields were to be left, and portions of vineyards, so that poor could harvest and provide for themselves basic necessities (Lev. 19:9-10). Generally, God directed that Israel be compassionate and caring in regard to the poor (Deut. 15:7-13; 24:19-22).
- Cheating a man out of his just wages was forbidden (Lev. 19:13; Deut. 24:14-15).
- Honest weights and measures were demanded so that the economy and commerce would not be undermined (Lev. 19:35-36; Deut. 25:13-17).
- Tithing (giving 10 percent) of all their production was required to underwrite the cost of maintaining the Levitical priesthood and caring for the poor (Deut. 14:22-29; 26:12-13).

### Using The Law Of Moses Today

Applying the principles found within the Law of Moses today creates some challenges. However, it is well worth the effort.

Many of the principles found in the law remain as relevant today as when they were presented to Israel. In fact, Jesus and other spokesmen in the New Testament repeat and expound upon many of them.

Some commandments must be examined carefully to determine whether they still apply or whether they addressed the unique "land covenant" made with Israel. It is not unusual to see Bible students reach different conclusions on such matters as debt, charging interest and forgiving debts (as in bankruptcy, etc.). So, we will need to be careful and aware of the differences in the old and new covenants, but nevertheless ready to observe eternal principles linking or transcending the covenants.

### ➢ Questions ◄

1. Are the material things of this world good or evil? Explain. _____
_____
_____
_____

2. What events in Abraham's life show he did not let wealth overcome his faith? _____
_____
_____
_____

3. In what ways did God bless Joseph for his faithfulness? _____
_____
_____
_____

4. Identify a lesson one can learn from Israel's exodus from Egypt concerning our exodus from sin. _____
_____
_____

5. Of the 10 Commandments, list the ones effecting one's wealth. _____

_____

_____

_____

_____

6. Should principles from the Law of Moses be considered when discussing the use of one's money/wealth today? Explain. _____

_____

_____

_____

_____

# GOD'S PROVISION:
# MANNA, CAPITAL, AND TITHING

Beyond the Pentateuch, the Old Testament continues to teach us valuable lessons about money and material things. Beginning in the book of Joshua, we read about Israel's conquest of Canaan and possession of the Promised Land, with God's strategic and vital assistance.

With the division of the land among the tribes (Joshua 14-22), Israel began an almost completely new existence. For forty years, the Israelites had been a nation of nomadic wanderers. They only possessed what they could carry and lived in the harsh wilderness environment in which other nations did not desire to live.

During this period, God sustained Israel directly, immediately, and miraculously. A nation of perhaps two or three million people would not have lasted long on the few animals they brought with them out of Egypt. Finding water, especially in a desert region, for that many people to drink, cook with, and bathe, was impossible without miraculous assistance.

God provided bread from heaven (manna) for Israel to eat, as well as quail and ample water supplies (Exod. 15:23-27; 16:4-36; 17:1-7; Num. 11:4-35; 20:2-13). In a general sense, God kept them free of disease (Exod. 15:26; 23:25). Even their clothes did not wear out during this journey (Deut. 29:5).

It is obvious God gave these provisions directly, immediately, and miraculously. Israel did not have to plant crops or harvest them. They did not have to dig wells or maintain them. All they had to do was go out and gather what God laid about their tents. This blessing of abundance without labor or earning effort would continue, but were destined to change in its character.

The Promised Land was an already mostly developed land. It is described as a "land flowing with milk and honey" (Exod. 3:8,17). It already had large and beautiful cities, abundant water, productive fields, houses, wells, vineyards, orchards and other natural resources (Deut. 6:10-11; 8:7-9; Josh. 24:13). God gave this to

> During this period, **God** sustained Israel **directly**, **immediately**, and **miraculously**.

He **expected** the nation to understand its **dependence** upon Him, but not to the exclusion of **individual effort**.

Israel. They did not have to work for it, beyond the effort of conquest, which also was minor when compared to God's part.

Once they possessed these things, the dynamic of God's provision changed. God had invested Israel with capital. He no longer simply laid each day's provisions at their doorstep, but instead had given them a portion of land and material goods with which they could sustain themselves.

God was not removed from the process, but His means of provision had changed. There are some important and relevant lessons in this for us today.

### The Concept Of Capital

Capital refers to wealth (land, other property, resources, or money) used to increase wealth. This was not unlike what God had done at the creation of the world. He had created and given to Adam and Eve all that was necessary for them to use to provide for themselves.

God took a group of people impoverished by slavery and gave them the capital for a new beginning. As Adam and Eve were to work in the garden (Gen. 1:28-30; 2:15) and use the physical capital God had given them to produce all they needed for daily living, so God did when he gave Israel the fully developed and resource-filled land of Canaan.

It is important to understand God expects us to both work and utilize the capital He has given us. We are to provide for ourselves and have what is necessary to help others.

During the temporary crisis period of the exodus, He sustained His people directly, but the ultimate purpose of God was to give each family a piece of land from which they could sustain themselves, help their neighbors and hand down an inheritance to their children.

### Personal Responsibility

This affirms the concept of personal responsibility in God's economic system for ancient Israel. He expected the nation to understand its dependence upon him, but not to the exclusion of individual effort. Israel became a co-laborer with God. This concept continues under the covenant of Christ.

Another way of approaching this concept is by comparing Israel's infancy and adulthood. In their infancy, God provided 24-hour a day provision in the wilderness when total dependency was a necessity. In Canaan in their adulthood, God expected them to remain dependent on Him, but He expected them to play a part in their prosperity.

As every parent knows, there are dangers in the transition from childhood to adulthood. God warned of this in Deuteronomy 8:10-17, saying, "When you have eaten and are full, then you shall bless the Lord your God for the good land which he has given you. Beware that you do not forget the Lord your God by not keeping his commandments, his judgments and his statutes which I command you today, lest—when you have eaten and are full, and have built beautiful houses and dwell in them; and when your herds and your flocks multiply, and your silver and your gold are multiplied, and all that you have is multiplied; when your heart is lifted up, and you forget the Lord your God, who brought you out of the land of Egypt, from the house of bondage...then you say in your heart, 'My power and the might of my hand have gained me this wealth.'"

Regarding capital, the key word is "multiply." God gave Israel land capital by which they could multiply their prosperity. Since He gave Israel the capital, they could not honestly claim to have accomplished their prosperity on their own. God was still the source of all their blessings.

### The Wisdom Of God In Capital

The New Testament teaches, "it is more blessed to give than to receive" (Acts 20:35). The full statement of the Apostle Paul was: "I have shown you in every way, by laboring like this, that you must support the weak. And remember the words of the Lord Jesus, that he said, 'It is more blessed to give than to receive.'"

By investing Israel with capital, God took them off the holy welfare system and provided them with the means of being more like God. By laboring and using their capital to increase their wealth, they now had the ability to give to others on a sustainable basis.

Many of the laws and regulations regarding care for the poor, the widow, and the orphan, which we studied in the last chapter, were to be underwritten by this capital-based economic system. No longer would God's people have to be primarily "receivers" of blessings. They now could be "givers" and giving is a divine characteristic.

### Dangers Inherent In Capitalism

We have already observed one danger. God warned against forgetting He gave the original capital. Other dangers include the temptation to consume all our capital produces with none left to help others, or to consume the capital itself and then be left unable to produce for the future.

The first consumption problem relates to a heart problem known as greed. Its solution is an inward change.

God legislated to avoid the second consumption problem—the loss of the primary capital itself. Under the Law of Moses, land lost through indebtedness was to be returned to its rightful heir twice a century during the Jubilee years. If obeyed, this law prevented a family ever completely losing their land capital (God's provision).

Another danger in capitalism is unwarranted accumulation. Men can become so wrapped up in the accumulation of wealth they forget its legitimate purposes. Hoarding and miserliness and covetousness are just a few of the sins produced when capitalism is divorced from its God-ordained purposes.

## Tithing: Rudimentary Principles On The Grace Of Giving

Tithing is the subject of much confusion and debate. Some see the term as merely equivalent to "giving." Others see it as God's continuing standard for the church today, even though the only recorded commandment to tithe God gave to Israel under the Mosaical covenant. Yet, others totally ignore tithing in understanding God's expectations in regard to Christian giving. All of these views fail, in some respect, to comprehend the valuable lessons found in the Old Testament tithing regulations.

It is accepted among many denominational preachers to proclaim tithing is the rule for the church today. Many claim to tithe, but the facts paint a different picture. The Barna Research Group has reported 17% of Americans claim to tithe, but only 6% actually do (Alcorn, 2003). It is hard to know whether these numbers reflect a misunderstanding of what tithing is, or whether it reflects dishonesty in reaction to pressures exerted within the denominational assemblies.

Tithing, by definition, involves the giving of a tenth or ten percent. Tithing refers to the amount of the offering. The term "firstfruits" refers to the nature of particular offerings—the first and the best.

The Old Testament tithe was not a voluntary or a freewill offering. It belonged to the Lord and was a commanded offering. Leviticus 27:30,32 says, "And all the tithe of the land, whether of the seed of the land or of the fruit of the tree, is the Lord's. It is holy to the Lord...And concerning the tithe of the herd or the flock, of whatever passes under the rod, the tenth one shall be holy to the Lord." Under the Law of Moses, giving any less was "robbing" God (Malachi 3:8-10). The law also spoke of a separate category of freewill offerings (Lev. 22:18-23; Num. 15:3; Deut. 12:6, 17). This was the type of offering given for the construction of the tabernacle in the wilderness (Exod. 35:29). Thus, we see voluntary gifts, the guiding principle of New Testament giving, did not begin with the new covenant. It co-existed with tithing under the Law of Moses.

The Patriarchs tithed before it was codified in the Law of Moses. Abraham offered tithes to God through Melchizedek, king and priest of Salem (Gen. 14:18-20; Heb. 7:1-10). This is the Bible's first record of tithing. Jacob also offered a tithe to the Lord before the nation of Israel existed (Gen. 28:22).

Mosaical tithing, besides its inherent worship aspect, served two primary purposes. (1) It supported the priesthood and temple. (2) It provided for the poor and needy.

Part of the tithes, as well as portions of most other sacrifices and offerings, were the inheritance of the Levites, since they did not receive a land possession in the Promised Land. The Levites then gave a tithe of what they received to the Lord (Num. 18:8-32). Another portion of the tithes was to provide for the needs of the stranger, the fatherless and the widow (Deut. 14:29).

### May Have Been Three Separate Tithes

While it is difficult to say so with absolute certainty, it appears God ordained three separate tithes: the tithe for the Levites (Num. 18:21-32), another for the sacred festivals (Deut. 12:17-18; 14:23), and another collected only every third year, for the orphans, widows, and poor (Deut. 14:28-29; 26:12-13).

If this is the case, then the faithful Israelite did not give merely ten percent of his prosperity, but more like twenty-three to twenty-four percent, not counting freewill offerings. Again, if this is true, it undermines the popular notion of a simple ten percent offering today mirroring the Old Testament practice or that such an amount is extremely generous by biblical standards.

Even brethren, who have argued if ten percent was the standard under the inferior covenant, then Christians should give more generously under the superior covenant, may have to recalibrate their measuring sticks. All of this really is moot because the New Testament nowhere commands tithing for Christians and the covenant and kingdom structures are quite different.

Israel was a theocracy, with God their ultimate governmental head. Much of what the tithes financed would be covered with regular government taxes today. The priesthood of Israel not only mediated for the people in worship and sacrifice, but served in a semi-legislative fashion when God's law needed to be clarified. Priests would use the Urim and Thummin to establish God's will, reporting the revelations to the people.

There was no divide in a theocracy between the religious and the secular. Thus, benevolent duties extended throughout the nation, since all were both physically and religiously "brethren."

We do not have this same situation in the church today. The kingdom of God exists within a variety of human governmental systems, and the demands upon the church are not the same as in Israel, though there are some parallels worth observing.

### Change Brought By New Covenant

It is no more credible to return to the Law of Moses for a pattern and authority for tithing than it is for animal sacrifice. Likewise, we do not look to the Law of Moses to authorize a Levitical priesthood or use of instrumental music in the worship of the church today.

We live under a new covenant and law. Through His death, Christ abolished the old law and covenant and replaced it with a better (Col. 2:13-17; Heb. 8:6-13). The New Testament neither commands tithing, nor gives us an example of such in the church.

Offerings received on the Lord's Day still underwrite the worship of the Lord, including provisions for those who dedicate their lives to leading the local church and preaching the word. However, there is no huge, separate priesthood and body of Levites to be supported today.

The church still has a duty to provide benevolence to a particular, but limited group of needy brethren. Yet, much of this responsibility is assigned to family members, not the church (1 Tim. 5:3-16). We will explore this in another lesson.

Freewill offerings are the rule of the New Testament (2 Cor. 8:12; 9:2,5,7). The New Testament teaches giving commensurate with prosperity. Tithing is one method of proportional giving. In the absence of tithing instructions under the Law of Christ, we are commanded to give as we have purposed in our hearts (2 Cor. 9:7), rather than following an established percentage.

With this in mind, Christians should contemplate whether they fulfill the command to give generously (2 Cor. 9:5-6)? It may be we give the typical three percent the IRS says Americans who itemize deductions report giving to church and charity.

The Apostle Paul wrote, "whatever things were written before were written for our learning" (Rom. 15:4). This is as true of what we read about tithing as about the other experiences of Israel recorded in scripture.

### What We Can Learn From Tithing

John C. Maxwell lists seven truths about tithing worth our attention (Maxwell, 1987). He illustrates these from what the Bible says in Deuteronomy 14:20—15:23.
1. Tithing was to be a regular exercise (14:22). It was to be done "year by year."
2. It also was a spiritual exercise (14:23). The tithe was to be eaten before the Lord in the place of his choosing. Thus, it was part of divinely ordained worship.
3. Tithing was a learned behavior (14:23). God said they were to tithe and sacrifice so they might learn to fear the Lord.
4. It also was a flexible exercise (14:24-26). If the place of worship was too far away to carry the tithe of grain or animals, God permitted exchanging them for money and bringing it to the Lord.
5. It was designed to be a joyful experience (14:26). The Israelites were to rejoice in the midst of their worshipful offerings.
6. Tithing was a beneficent activity (14:27-29). As previously noted, the tithe benefited the Levites, priests, and the poor, widowed, and orphaned.
7. Tithing was a blessed exercise (14:29). God connected his blessing upon their work to their faithful tithing.

While Maxwell appears in his writing to incorrectly assume tithing remains the standard for giving in the New Testament church, the seven truths he identifies concerning tithing are applicable to the giving as we are prospered in the church age. Tithing certainly demonstrates giving was a part of worship under the Law of Moses, just as it is under the Law of Christ.

There are other principles learned through the older model of tithing equally true of Christian offerings. Giving under both systems helps us learn to put God first. Both systems require us to count our blessings and calculate the portion to be offered to the Lord. Under either method, the worshipper is reminded all we have is from God, and through our offerings, we can communicate our gratitude for his generosity.

### Cited

Alcorn, R. (2003). *Money, possessions, and eternity.* (p. xi). Wheaton, IL.: Tyndale House Publishers.

Maxwell, J.C. (1987). *Deuteronomy, the communicator's commentary.* Waco, TX.: Word Book Publisher.

### ➢ Questions ◄

1. When leaving Egypt, what did God expect Israel to learn from His directly, immediately, and miraculously giving of their daily provisions? _____
_____
_____
_____

2. Once in the land of Canaan, what did God expect Israel to learn when He blessed them with the material goods to sustain themselves? _____
_____
_____

3. Considering God's provisions to Israel leaving Egypt versus dwelling in Canaan, what are some lessons parents might learn in teaching their children about material possessions? _____
_____
_____
_____

4. What are some dangers in capitalism? _____
_____
_____
_____

5. List three purposes tithing served. _____
_____
_____
_____
_____

6. How did changing the covenants affect one's giving to God? _____
_____
_____
_____

# BIBLE WISDOM ABOUT MONEY

As we explore what the Bible says about money and related issues, we do well to investigate the "wisdom literature" of the Old Testament. Included in this category of Scripture are the books of Job, Psalms, Proverbs, Ecclesiastes and the Song of Solomon. The latter three are largely the work of Solomon, renowned for his wisdom.

These books largely focus on practical issues related to godly living in this world. So, it is not surprising money issues are, directly and indirectly, addressed in each.

### Proverbs

If a person wants to learn how to prosper materially and financially, how to manage his assets, and keep them in proper perspective, few books contain more wisdom in such matters than the Proverbs. This book teaches how to protect oneself against the extremes of wealth and poverty, which is a recurring biblical theme. It addresses both outward issues regarding money and possessions, as well as the inward issues of the heart.

Reading through all the proverbs, one will be amazed at the sheer volume of poetic teaching on these matters. Let us be sure we understand the nature of proverbs. They are "general truths" about various matters. They are not promises. There are exceptions to the general rule. This fact does not negate the golden kernels of truth about money, its acquisition, and its maintenance.

Here is a sampling of relevant teachings on our subject in proverbial form:
• All wealth comes from God (10:22).
• Humility and fear of the Lord result in wealth (3:9-10; 22:4).
• Riches are, to a great degree, a by-product of godly wisdom (3:16; 24:3-4).
• Wisdom more valuable than gold (8:1-21).

**God rewards** particular human activity, including but not limited to diligent **work**, **generosity**, and **trust in Him**.

"There is one who makes himself **rich**, yet has **nothing**; and one who makes himself **poor**, yet has **great riches**" (Pro. 13:7)

- Riches themselves not evil, but the inordinate desire for them (23:4-5; 28:20).
- Riches often tempt us to deny God, or our need for him (30:8-9).
- Being industrious produces prosperity while laziness and hastiness bring poverty (6:10-11; 10:4; 12:11; 14:23; 15:19; 18:9; 19:15; 21:5, 25; 27:23-24; 31:27).
- Work is the primary tool for generating wealth (12:11; 13:4).
- Righteousness and evil are repaid in kind (13:21,25).
- Righteousness is better than wealth (15:6; 16:8; 28:6).
- Better to be poor and righteous than rich and evil (15:16-17; 16:8; 19:1; 28:6).
- Inherited money, as opposed to that worked for, often is quickly lost (20:21).
- Those with possessions need to help the needy; giving to needy is "lending to the Lord" (3:27-28; 11:24-25; 19:17; 21:13; 22:9; 28:27; 29:7; 31:20).
- Money and wealth are not inherently good; there are better things (3:13-16; 8:10-11; 16:16; 17:1).
- Do not overwork or be greedy; material things are transitory; moderation is the best course (1:19; 23:4-5; 30:8-9).
- Wealth will bring you a lot of "friends" (19:4; 14:20).
- Slow, steady accumulation is a better approach than hasty speculation (21:5).
- Riches are no substitute for righteousness in judgment (11:4, 28).
- Warnings against oppressing the poor (14:31; 22:22-23).
- Need to save and not squander resources; anticipate future needs (6:6-8; 21:20).
- Do not trust in riches (11:28; 28:25).
- Investing shown a wise means of increasing wealth (31:16).
- Dishonest gain condemned (11:1; 16:11; 20:10, 17, 23; 21:6).
- Inheritances: their benefits and perils (13:22; 20:21).
- Under the Old Covenant, future prosperity tied to returning proper share to the Lord and generosity to others (3:9-10; 11:24-26). Tithe belonged to God (Malachi 3:8-12).
- Some poverty is created by personal foolishness (20:4; 21:17; 23:20-21; 24:30-34).
- Be careful of debt, it can enslave (22:7).
- Be careful for whom you co-sign as a guarantee for payment of a debt (6:1-5; 11:15; 17:18; 22:26-27). Do not guarantee what you cannot afford to pay.

We might summarize by saying God is the source of all our material and financial blessings. Gaining wealth through God's blessing is not a passive activity. God rewards particular human activity, including but not limited to diligent work, generosity, and trust in Him. If it comes down to a decision between being rich and sinful or poor and righteous, the latter is the best choice.

Further, we see not all rich people will be blessed in the long run. Sinful riches are actually quite costly. On the other hand, we learn not all poverty is equal. Some poverty is inadvertent, while other cases result from sinful indulgence or lack of personal effort.

Riches are best when viewed like happiness—a byproduct of doing what is right. When one pursues riches or happiness as a goal, neither is obtained.

Money is a powerful tool for good in the hands of the wise. Leave God and righteousness out of the equation, and it becomes the opposite.

There are enigmas in regard to money also explored in Proverbs. "There is one who makes himself rich, yet has nothing; and one who makes himself poor, yet has great riches" (13:7). "There is one who scatters, yet increases more; and there is one who withholds more than is right, but it leads to poverty" (11:24). These speak to the issue of greed or hoarding resulting in the loss of what the person most wants.

### The Book Of Job

The case of Job is best remembered for its lessons about human suffering. As we look carefully at the story of Job, we find some important things about physical possessions and their relative value, as well.

If the Proverbs teach us the "general truth" about acquiring wealth, then the book of Job teaches us about the "exceptions" to these general rules. Not every faithful child of God lives in material prosperity.

The Bible introduces Job to us as a very righteous man who was also very wealthy (Job 1:1-3). Like Abraham, David and Solomon, God blessed him with great material possessions, in part because of his faithfulness. Part of Job's righteousness was he used his material blessings to help the less fortunate and did not trust in his wealth (Job 29:12-16; 31:16-28).

The heart of the book's message evolves from a challenge made by Satan to God concerning Job. Satan argues Job is faithful to God only because God made obedience "pay" by all the blessings He bestowed on the ancient patriarch (Job 1:9-11; 2:4-6). The issue is what Job loves: God or his possessions.

What follows is the account of a two-phase test of Job's integrity, administered by Satan, but limited by God. We tend to focus more on the second phase, where Job's health is brought to the brink of death, and he lives in dire misery. Let us not forget the first phase of his test.

By giving Job so much prosperity, Satan alleged God effectively "bought" Job's faithfulness and built such a protective hedge around him Job had little choice but to obey the Lord. "Does Job fear God for nothing?" Satan asks. He asserts if God will reach out and "touch all that he has," Job will curse Him  (Job 1:9-11).

Quickly we learn Satan was wrong in his first accusation. God permits the cataclysmic and sudden removal of everything Job had, including his livestock, servants, and children. Remember, in these ancient times, a man's wealth was measured in terms of his herds and flocks, not money in the bank.

Job is famous for his answer to all this disaster. "Naked I came from my mother's womb, and naked shall I return there. The Lord gave, and the Lord has taken away; blessed be the name of the Lord" (Job 1:21). Job determined to depend upon God, not his prosperity.

A couple of lessons are worth noting here:
• Job's faith and obedience were not dependent on God physically blessing him. Satan's allegation Job would serve God only as long as obedience paid material dividends was proved wrong.
• Job understood the source of his wealth was God. If the Lord saw wisdom in giving him much, he determined to bless God. On the other hand, if the Lord saw purpose in removing Job's wealth, he also would defer to God's sovereignty and bless Him.

At the conclusion of the book of Job, after the patriarch faithfully survived not only losing his wealth, but his health, God restored both, giving him even greater material goods (Job 42:10-13). In fact, God doubled his assets.

The great emotional struggles Job experienced were focused primarily on the excruciating physical suffering he endured. With regard to his prosperity, he foreshadowed in his behavior the attitude expressed many generations later by the Apostle Paul. "I have learned in whatever state I am, to be content: I know how to be abased, and I know how to abound" (Phil. 4:11-12).

The case of Job demonstrates the fallacy of "health and wealth gospels," both promised to those who serve God. Such false teaching grossly over-simplifies the Bible message about material prosperity and ignores God's providential use of suffering and need. Good men do not always prosper and evil men do not always suffer in this world (Job 21:7-21; 24:1-12). Unseen forces, divine or demonic, are at work in ways we cannot always see or understand.

## Ecclesiastes

In this book of wisdom, Solomon explores life's purpose and meaning from two perspectives, with and without God and His will in the picture. He concludes life, no matter how comfortably lived, is mere "vanity," an useless endeavor without a spiritual perspective. He concludes his whole investigation and poetic treatise by declaring, "Let us hear the conclusion of the whole matter: Fear God and keep his commandments, for this is man's all" (12:13).

What is most interesting for our study in this book is Solomon speaks of having explored these issues through personal experience. God blessed him with riches beyond all other kings and kingdoms of his day, and a level of wealth beyond our imagination. Solomon is particularly qualified to write on issues related to money, wealth and possessions.

While Solomon spoke by inspiration, he also spoke from experience. He had experiences unlike us. He speaks of having virtually unlimited resources to pursue comfort, pleasure, accomplishment and honor, and he writes of the problems and limitations of earthly wealth and possessions.

Each of the first 10 chapters contains teaching about money-related issues. This is a major component of "the words of the Preacher."

## Life And Physical Blessings To Be Enjoyed

Solomon repeatedly declares the product of our work, including money and wealth, should be enjoyed as blessings from God (3:12-13; 5:18-19; 7:14; 8:15; 9:7, 9). Wealth is not evil in itself. Solomon had wisely asked God for wisdom at the beginning of his reign, and God gave him his request, plus great wealth (1 Kings 3:7-14; 2 Chron. 1:7-12). If God gives something, it cannot be inherently evil.

1 Kings 10 and 2 Chronicles 9 discusses the scope of Solomon's wealth. His palatial house and other amenities of kingship are described in both these books.

Wisdom and money are "defenses" against many of the troubles and problems of life, but wisdom is the greater of these (7:12). In the long run, a smaller accumulation of possessions and a quiet life are better than great possessions and an unsettled desire for more and more (4:5).

## Wealth Never Satisfies

Solomon states material things never satisfy, the eye never sees enough, and the ear never hears enough (1:8). He said a man who loves silver will never be satisfied with the amount he has (5:10). Happiness cannot be purchased. In chapter 2, Solomon tells how he explored many avenues seeking pleasure, happiness, and satisfaction. He gratified his fleshly desires to levels none of us could even attempt. He had multiple mansions, vineyards, orchards, gardens, immense herds and flocks, and innumerable servants to help him with it all. He had gold and so much silver it became as common as stones (1 Kings 10:27). He said, "Whatever my eyes desired I did not keep from them. I did not withhold my heart from any pleasure" (2:10).

He found working and doing good are essential to a meaningful life. Merely having money and all the things it can buy does not make a person happy.

## Problems Accompanying Money And Wealth

- All men will die and leave behind the product of their work. What does one gain from their effort if God and eternity are not in the picture (1:3)? Will the people who inherit our things be wise or foolish (2:18)? Will they use it the way we would have done, or squander it like the Prodigal Son (Luke 15)? In any case, we will be leaving it to someone who did not "earn" it with their own labor (2:21).
- Like many today, Solomon found financial success often results in friends and neighbors becoming envious (4:4). Instead of bringing happiness, wealth can bring division, sadness, and worse.
- Solomon found the more wealth he had the more servants he had to maintain to take care of it all (5:11). Today, when we buy more cars, boats, campers, cabins, computers, televisions, and the like, we have the expense and worry of maintaining, insuring, housing, and paying taxes on it all.
- The laboring man of poor or modest means can sleep peacefully, but the wealthy have worries or concerns related to their possessions often making sleep difficult (5:12).
- Riches can be lost (6:2). If one is overly dependent upon them for happiness and a sense of well-being, then such a loss becomes a disaster. If one is more focused on God, doing good, and the spiritual component of life, the lost riches are just lost riches.

## All Things Must Be Kept In There Place

One of Solomon's more quoted statements is, "To everything there is a season, a time for every purpose under heaven" (3:1). He then elaborates with a plethora of examples.

There are many applications of this principle, but we certainly should learn work, money, possessions, and pleasure all have their time and place. They must be kept in their proper place and balance. Greed and all its attendant sins develop when this perspective is lost (1 Tim. 6:9-10).

Work is important, but not the only thing in life. What has one gained if he works so much he cannot enjoy the product of his work? On the other hand, as in the Proverbs, Ecclesiastes warns against the adverse effects of laziness or idleness (10:18).

## Money Must Be Properly Used

Ecclesiastes emphasizes enjoying God's blessings, but also focuses on keeping God in the picture as we do. When one uses money and possessions to do "good," he finds happiness. When the same things are used merely to gratify the flesh or build some sort of sense of security, happiness and wellbeing are illusive.

Also, Solomon emphasizes the vanity and often harm in keeping or hoarding wealth—not actually using it for some good purpose (5:13-16). Again, all men die. If we do not use our blessings while living, they have no value to us when we are dead. Hoarding is an extreme, just as is wasting. Neither is a wise use of money.

### The Psalms

The Psalms do not have nearly as much material in them about wealth, money, and possessions as do the Proverbs or Ecclesiastes. Some psalms touch on our subject.

For instance, Psalm 49 speaks of the folly of trusting or boasting in one's wealth. It is temporary in nature. When one dies, it is left to another. In verses 7-12, the psalmist shows worldly wealth produces spiritual blindness. He fails to realize money cannot buy the salvation of the soul. Peter made the same point in the New Testament (1 Peter 1:18-19). Under the Old Testament law, under certain circumstances, a man could purchase his own life. A sentence of death could be reduced to a fine (Exodus 21:28-29). In such cases, wealth could deliver one from death, but only when men were dealing with men. There never was any way of purchasing a life forfeited to God.

Further, a man might be able to use money to bribe a judge, but never death. Verse 13 suggests wealth can lead to spiritual folly or foolishness.

Psalm 37 emphasizes trusting in the Lord results in physical prosperity as well as spiritual blessing. Those who wait on the Lord will inherit the earth. Verse 25 suggests beggars will be rare among God's people. "I have been young, and now am old; Yet I have not seen the righteous forsaken, nor his descendants begging bread."

While the direct involvement of providence may be in view here, it also is likely the principles of righteousness, such as industriousness, good stewardship, prudence, circumspection, and self-control also play a large role. The duty of fellow righteous people to help their brethren in need must not be overlooked in the total picture.

Psalm 112 approaches wealth as a blessing from God, but demonstrates the godly man so blessed will be gracious, compassionate, and full of righteousness. Thus, the godly man lends to those in need, helps the poor, and is generous and wise in the use of his possessions.

The last three verses of Psalm 144 relate human prosperity to trusting and serving the Lord, a common Old Testament theme.

## Song of Solomon

This book is generally deemed to extol the beauty of human love and, perhaps, designed as a type of the relationship of Christ and the church. It has little in it directly related to the issue of money and possessions.

Some have seen in its pages two suitors for the hand of the Shulamite maiden—the king and a young shepherd boy. They see the maiden choosing the love of the poorer shepherd over the riches available by marrying the king. If this interpretation has validity, then the superior value of love over riches may be seen.

Other interpretations do not see two men vying for the Shulamite's hand, and thus there is little in the book on our subject, with that perspective.

## ➢ Questions ◁

1. From Proverbs, why is righteousness better than wealth? _____
   _____
   _____
   _____

2. In what way are the physical blessings of the Lord not a passive activity on the part of the individual? _____
   _____
   _____

3. How did Satan tempt Job to be unfaithful to God? Is this a temptation for some today?
   _____
   _____
   _____
   _____

4. In what way did Job fulfill the words of Paul from Philippians 4:11-12? _____
   _____
   _____
   _____
   _____

5. From Ecclesiastes, identify at least two problems that accompany money and wealth. Explain how these problems can interfere with one's service to God. ___

---------------------------------------------------------------------------------
---------------------------------------------------------------------------------
---------------------------------------------------------------------------------
---------------------------------------------------------------------------------
---------------------------------------------------------------------------------

6. According to Psalm 112, what is the source of one's wealth? How does a godly person use their wealth? _____

_____
_____
_____
_____
_____

# HOW THE PROPHETS ADDRESSED SOCIO-ECONOMICS ISSUES

Israel had begun its existence as a nation of poor peasants, recently freed slaves. For the first forty years of their existence, every portion of their prosperity was directly a gift from God. The culmination of God's ten plagues on Egypt included not only Israel's freedom, but also their carrying away of the wealth of Egypt (Exod. 12:35-36).

Upon entering the Promised Land in the second generation, each Israelite was on an equal standing, each receiving his own portion of the land of Canaan. Beginning in the period of the judges, things began to change. Instead of obeying God and exterminating the idolatrous peoples of Canaan completely, we read, "And it came to pass, when Israel was strong, that they put the Canaanites under tribute, but did not completely drive them out" (Judges 1:28). Notice the people decided to collect money from those they conquered instead of driving them out or killing them. This set the stage for Israel being influenced by the ungodly economic and religious practices of the heathens.

The rest of the book of Judges presents a series of cycles. Each begins with Israel turning away from God's commandments. God's reaction each time is removal of His protection and His blessings, resulting in a loss of both freedom and economic prosperity. When the situation worsened, Israel would repent and plead to God for help. Each time God raised up a deliverer (judge) who restored freedom, safety, and prosperity. Then, when people forgot, the cycle repeated itself.

### Desire For Earthly King Brought New Economic Problems

God's people have nearly always struggled to be satisfied with a heavenly king. The system of government God introduced under both the Old and New Covenants has central government headquartered in heaven.

In ancient Israel, this system prevailed through the periods of Moses, Joshua, and the judges. The people yearned for a

> **Woe** to those who **join** house to house; they **add** field to field, till there is **no place** where they may dwell alone in the midst of the land" (Isaiah 5:8).

visible, earthly monarch. Notice, "we also may be like all the nations, and that our king may judge us and go out before us and fight our battles" (1 Sam. 8:20).

God predicted and planned for this (Deut. 17:14-20). When Israel rejected the leadership of both Samuel and God, the Lord told Samuel to tell the nation what to expect from an earthly king. Samuel told Israel to expect their sons to be drafted into standing armies (taking them away from working in crops and flocks). Others would be drafted into other forms of service to support the earthly government. Further, he told them to expect confiscation of the best of their fields, vineyards and groves for the king's servants, as well as heavy taxation (1 Sam. 8:10-18).

All of this came to pass. Through the reigns of Saul, David, and Solomon, the economic burdens of earthly government continuously increased. At the death of Solomon and the ascension of Rehoboam to the throne, the people cried out, "Your father made our yoke heavy; now therefore, lighten the burdensome service of your father," (1 Kings 12:4). Rehoboam refused, promising "whereas my father put a heavy yoke on you, I will add to your yoke..." (1 Kings 12:11). This is, in part, the reason the kingdom divided.

**God's pattern** for kingdom government is not only **perfect** in its rule, but **economically efficient**.

People still complain about the cost of government and taxes today. Interestingly, the principle also maintains in the church. Denominations, insisting on a centralized earthly government (popes, synods, councils, etc.), find the economic cost of maintaining these high.

Whether it is the earthly kings of Israel or the demand for an earth-based central church government, both were and are destined to fail, in spite of the huge economic costs. God's pattern for kingdom government is not only perfect in its rule, but economically efficient.

### Economic Sins Sharply Divided Israel Into Classes

By the time of the divided kingdom and due to sinful use of material prosperity, some of God's people had begun to live in luxury, while others lived in terrible poverty. Every economic and social sin God had warned against in the giving of the law and covenant began to appear.

God sent prophets to the people of the divided kingdom over a period of hundreds of years. One of the messages of these prophets was a denunciation of extortion, unjust weights in commerce, oppression of the poor, defrauding men of their wages, and using positions of religious authority to make themselves rich.

The Lord had given every family in Israel a portion (heritage) in the Promised Land. Handled in a godly manner, it would produce an abundance and great wealth for each family. Jeremiah spoke for God saying, "I brought you into a bountiful country, to eat its fruit and its goodness. But when you entered, you defiled my land and made my heritage an abomination" (Jer. 2:7). Isaiah described the dissatisfaction with God's provision and how greed enriched some and impoverished others. He said, "Woe to those who join house to house; they add field to field, till there is no place where they may dwell alone in the midst of the land" (Isaiah 5:8).

"Indeed, the prophetic denunciation against Israel can be connected directly with the development of class distinctions under the monarchy, the appearance of a commercial, moneyed class and the growth of a patriciate who lived a life of luxury and self-indulgence and gave not a thought to the miseries of the poor who toiled for them," wrote N.W. Porteous (Porteous, 1966).

### Sins Of Israel With Respect To Material Possessions

It is probably impossible to make an exhaustive list of all of Israel's sins related to money and possessions. Many such sins were interlinked with other types of sin. The following is at least a substantial sampling of the sins God sent the prophets to condemn.

- Worshipping idols made of costly materials, such as gold and silver—Isaiah 2:7-8, 20.
- Extortion, robbery, and oppression to gain more land—Ezekiel 22:29; Micah 2:2; Amos 5:11-12.
- Corrupt business practices, including dishonest scales and prices—Ezekiel 45:10-12; Hosea 12:7.
- Foreclosing on unpaid debts by taking even a man's clothing for payment—Amos 2:6-8.
- Cheating laborers of their wages—Malachi 3:5.
- Ignoring holy days or chafing because they impeded commerce—Amos 8:5.
- Living in excessive luxury while others suffered—Amos 6:4-6.
- Religious and political leaders corrupted, acted for personal economic gain rather than in righteousness—Micah 3:11, 7:3; Isaiah 3:14-15, Jeremiah 6:13, 8:10.
- Bribery, usury, and even murder common—Ezekiel 22:6-12.
- Robbing God of offerings and tithes—Malachi 3:8-10.

Amos may have been the prophet who most clearly defined the economic sins of Israel before God's judgment on the nation. He described the luxurious life of the rich: with splendid houses (3:15; 5:11; 6:11), vineyards (5:11), wine and feasts (4:1; 6:5-6; 8:10), and a false sense of security (6:1).

"It was not luxury itself that caused him to announce the downfall of the nation. The main sins for which he denounced the wealthy, apart from a rare reference to the practice of idolatrous worship (5:25-26; 8:14), were of three kinds, all characteristic of a class that knew no restraint and could apparently behave as it pleased; unjust treatment of the poor (including robbery and violence), insincere worship and commercial dishonesty. These three were closely linked," wrote R. Norman Whybray (Whybray, 2002).

The link with worship is evidenced in Amos 8:5 where the prophet said the people of Israel whined, "When will the New Moon be past that we may sell grain? And the Sabbath that we may trade wheat?" Like so many today, the people of Israel chafed at having to take a day off from making money to honor and worship the God Who gave them all their blessings.

A study of Israel's sins in the days of the prophets helps us today to see sins involving money and possessions. They are interlinked with sins related to worship, justice, sexual morality, and many more. The words of the prophets help us to see the underlying thoughts of the heart leading to such sins.

The moral and economic sins of Israel completely corrupted the entire social order. The prophets rejected as doomed the society they observed in their days. "They did so because the social order they knew embodied a wrong view of life in society, supported false values, and sought its security and satisfactions from wrong sources and by mistaken methods. Political forms, economic activities, legal and judicial practice, social institutions, public morals, culture and religion—all were deformed by a basic error as to the meaning, values and direction of life," wrote R.B.Y. Scott (Scott, 1978).

It is important to read the writings of the prophets in the context of the times in which they wrote. However, it is impossible not to see the relevance of many of their messages for the age in which we live.

### Israel's History Typical

The history of Israel demonstrates what often happens in the lives of individuals today. When men and women are poor, they tend to feel more dependent upon God and less prone to the sins of pride, arrogance, and self-sufficiency.

While prosperity is a blessing from God, sin always results when men lose sight of this and become arrogant in assuming by their own wisdom and labor they prospered. Sin grows worse and worse. God said through Hosea, "I knew you in the wilderness, in the land of great drought. When they had pasture, they were filled; they were filled and their heart was exalted; therefore they forgot me" (Hosea 13:5-6).

Isaiah expressed the need for a drastic change in Israel's socio-economic behavior. He wrote, "Is this not the fast that I have chosen: to loose the bonds of wickedness, to undo the heavy burdens, to let the oppressed go free, and that you break every yoke? Is it not to share your bread with the hungry, and that you bring to your house the poor who are cast out; when you see the naked, that you cover him, and not hide yourself from your own flesh?" (Isaiah 58:6-7).

God promised to punish the selfishness, greed, and covetousness. "Therefore they have become great and grown rich. They have grown fat, they are sleek; yes, they surpass the deeds of the wicked; they do not plead the cause, the cause of the fatherless; yet they prosper, and the right of the needy they do not defend. Shall I not punish them for these things? Says the Lord. Shall I not avenge myself on such as nation as this?" (Jer. 5:27-29).

God did punish the nation, letting ten tribes be carried away into Assyrian captivity and later the southern kingdom into Babylonian exile. A remnant returned to rebuild Jerusalem and the temple in the days of Persian rule under the guidance of men like Zerubbabel, Ezra, and Nehemiah. Even unto the coming of Jesus, the nation never again enjoyed the unparalleled physical blessings enjoyed initially in the days of Joshua and the first kings of Israel.

When Jesus came into the world, the Jewish people were mostly a suffering people. Thus, the words of the Lord resonated with many and huge throngs initially followed him. Likewise, as the church was established on Pentecost and brethren cared for one another's needs, this godly approach to life and dependence upon the Lord's blessings drew thousands.

Evangelism has virtually always been more successful in times of economic depression and among the poorer people of the world. At present, this is illustrated in the unusually rapid spread of the gospel in the Philippines. Conversely, when nations are prosperous and imagine themselves self-sufficient, evangelism is very difficult. This is well illustrated throughout Europe and North America.

### Cited

Porteous, N.W. (1966). *Service in Christ*. Grand Rapids, MI: Eerdman's Publishing Co., (article title: "The Care of the Poor in the Old Testament").
Whybray, R.N. (2002). *The good life in the old testament*. (p. 266). London and New York: T&T Clark Ltd.
Scott, R.B.Y. (1978). *The relevance of the prophets*. (Revised ed., p. 172). New York, NY: The Macmillian Company.

### ➤ Questions ◄

1. When Israel began to possess Canaan, what effects did putting the Canannites under tribute have on their relationship with God and their daily lives? _____
   _____
   _____
   _____

2. How was Israel affected economically by their decision to replace God's leadership with their own? _____
   _____
   _____
   _____
   _____

3. List some ways Israel turned God's heritage into an abomination. _____
   _____
   _____
   _____
   _____

4. In what ways are the writings of the prophets relevant today. _____
   _____
   _____
   _____
   _____

5.  Even though prosperity if from the Lord, why is it dangerous (as in the case of Israel)?

_____

_____

_____

# JESUS' TEACHING ABOUT ECONOMIC ISSUES / ATTITUDES

Jesus' teaching about money and possessions can be perplexing and upsetting to the mindset of Americans today. As a result, many who read His words struggle for the true meaning and applications. This is good because, as we struggle to learn what Jesus is saying, we have to examine much more than our checkbooks and bank accounts. This subject is so critical because its roots reach down into every attitude and emotion of the heart.

Jesus spoke a great deal about money matters. No subject other than the kingdom of God itself drew more of His attention, according to the gospel records. Nearly half of Jesus' parables focused on economic issues or used them to teach other spiritual truths.

### Money Messages On The Mount

There are different views regarding the Lord's famous Sermon on the Mount. Some view it as the basic principles of discipleship or the constitution of the kingdom. Others see it as a call to radical reformation. It is probably all of these and much more.

As Jesus introduces the heart of His preaching in this mountain-side sermon to the masses, He gives us some basic insights into His views about money, its uses, and misuses.

### Money And Worship

Material gifts to God are a part of worshipping God. Whether it was the firstfruits of harvests in the Old Testament or our weekly giving on the Lord's Day under the New Testament, they reflect our acknowledgement of God as the source of all our blessings and our desire to have fellowship in the work of His kingdom. It is a form of sacrifice when done properly.

Early in His sermon, Jesus illustrated gifts to God are not acceptable if sin separates us from our brethren. He said, "Therefore if you bring your gift to the altar, and there remember that your brother has something against you, leave your gift there before

When a **Christian** puts his focus on **God** and righteousness and quits worrying about the future he cannot see anyway, **extraordinary** things **happen**. When we quit worrying about keeping up with the Jones, then we often see **the truth** of **Jesus' words** in very practical ways.

the altar, and go on your way. First be reconciled to your brother, and then come and offer your gift" (Matt. 5:23-24). This makes relatively clear external elements of worship, including our gifts, fail in their intent if our relationships with God and those created in His image are flawed by sin.

Developing on this theme, Jesus continued, "Take heed that you do not do your charitable deeds before men, to be seen by them. Otherwise you have no reward from your Father in heaven. Therefore, when you do a charitable deed, do not sound a trumpet before you as the hypocrites do in the synagogue and in the streets, that they may have glory from men. Assuredly, I say to you, they have their reward. But when you do a charitable deed, do not let your left hand know what your right hand is doing, that your charitable deed may be in secret; and your Father who sees in secret will Himself reward you openly" (Matt. 6:1-4).

Jesus previously had described His disciples as the "light of the world" and the "salt of the earth." He commanded this light not be hid, but shined so those who see these good works may glorify the Father in heaven (Matt. 5:13-16).

What Jesus addresses is not a demand for total secrecy in our good deeds and charity, but our intent. If we use gifts of money or other things merely to attract honor and glory to ourselves, we have failed. However, if men see our good works and honor God, then we have been faithful disciples and servants of the Lord.

An example of what Jesus was concerned about developed in the early church. In Acts 2:44-45, the earliest Christians sold possessions and distributed to the needs of other Christians. Men like Barnabas sold land and publicly laid the proceeds at the feet of the apostles for distribution to needy saints (Acts 4:34-37). However, in the next chapter of Acts, we read of a couple named Ananias and Sapphira, who sold land and gave a portion of it, leaving the impression they had given all. They were not required to give all of it, but apparently wanted to appear to men to be doing the same as Barnabas and others. They were struck dead for this hypocritical deception. They appear to have been more interested in the glory and praise than in actually helping fellow saints (Acts 5:1-11).

When Jesus instructed not to let the left hand know what the right hand was doing, He likely was using hyperbole (an exaggeration to make a point). Such is not literally possible. Total secrecy is not intended as is evident in the next and parallel discussion of prayer (Matt. 6:5-8). Jesus did not there imply all prayers must be secret, any more than all giving must be secret. He was addressing pretentious, hypocritical prayer. Jesus Himself prayed publicly (Mark 8:6; 14:22-23; Luke 21:17; John 11:41-42; 17:1-26). Further, we notice Jesus did not condemn people He observed giving gifts publicly. The widow with her two mites is one example. Jesus watched her and others putting their offerings into the treasury (Luke 21:1-4).

**Earthly Treasures vs. Heavenly Treasures**

Jesus instructed, "Do not lay up for yourselves treasures on earth, where moth and rust destroy and where thieves break in and steal; but lay up for yourselves treasures in heaven, where neither moth nor rust destroys and where thieves do not break in and steal. For where your treasure is, there your heart will be also" (Matt. 6:19-21).

These words of the Lord evoke serious, sometimes troubling introspections in dutiful saints. "What kind of treasure am I storing up?" asks the concerned disciple. The answer is not always easy to find.

Jesus was not here condemning all accumulation of wealth, for the Bible records a number of righteous men and women who had great wealth and used it for the furtherance of God's purposes and kingdom (Abraham, David, Joseph of Arimathea, Barnabas, Lydia). It would not seem Jesus was condemning reasonable work and planning ahead because many of the proverbs of the Old Testament encouraged such (Prov. 6:6-8; 10:5; 13:22; 21:5). He did warn against being overly concerned about tomorrow (Matt. 6:25-34).

He is more concerned, in His discussion of treasure, about the focus of a person's life, what constitutes their main objectives and goals. Is it earthly accumulation or eternal reward? The truth is a rich man may be laying up treasure in heaven while a poor man may be totally focused on earthly accumulation (even though he has little). Of course, the opposite can be true.

Jesus further illustrated His point on another occasion, when He told the parable of the wealthy and foolish farmer who trusted for the future in his bulging barns. God called him a fool because that night his soul was to be taken and all his possessions suddenly would belong to another. He had laid up earthly treasures but had not been "rich toward God" (Luke 12:16-21).

When Jesus summarized by saying our treasure is dependent upon our heart, He pinpointed the issue. The heart is the center of our mental and moral activity. Treasures are our dearest possessions. So, our "treasures" are dependent upon what our heart determines is dearest or most important to us. Is it earthly wealth or spiritual accomplishment?

What is it we treasure most? To help answer this question, answer the following ones.
- What do I think about the most?
- What occupies most of my emotional and physical energy?
- How do I respond when I see another human being's need?
- How do I react to sermons and lessons on the use of my material possessions?
- What are my priorities, beyond making and accumulating money and possessions?
- When I do give, what is my attitude about that giving?

**Cannot Serve Two Masters**

Continuing the thought in His sermon that disciples must make choices and establish priorities when it comes to money and possessions, Jesus said, "No one can serve two masters; for either he will hate the one and love the other, or else he will be loyal to the one and despise the other. You cannot serve God and mammon" (Matt. 6:24). Jesus exploded the myth one can pursue, as a goal,

If men **see** our **good works** and **honor God**, we have been faithful **disciples** and **servants** of the Lord.

earthly wealth and still be a servant of God. He declares you cannot do both. You cannot serve both.  Mammon is, more or less, the god of money.

Again, the issue is not necessarily whether you have wealth, but what role it plays in the priorities of your life. Is wealth a goal and objective of your life, seen as the ticket to happiness, comfort, and security? Is living to please God and serve His objectives your goal? If the latter is the case and you use your prosperity to that end, money is your servant and not the other way around.

Most of us probably would be quick to place ourselves in the latter category. Let us not move on too quickly. Jesus' teaching and our self-assessments cannot be so easily considered and dismissed. To illustrate this, the scripture tells of a rich young man who came to Jesus with the express purpose of finding out what he needed to do to inherit eternal life. The scriptures tell us he was a moral man who kept God's commandments. Jesus told him the only thing remaining for him was to sell all he had and give it to the poor. The young man went away sorrowful, apparently unwilling to give up his great wealth to obtain eternal life (Matt. 19:16-22).

Jesus was not instructing all disciples must dispose of all their wealth, but He perceived this young man, though interested in eternal life, was more interested in his earthly possessions. The young man's sorrowful departure appears to have confirmed this.

If you had the young rich man's choice, what decision would you really make?

## Do Not Worry So Much About Making Money

If we do not put a priority on making money and accumulating some reserves, how are we going to have food, clothing, and shelter? Jesus answers this dilemma too, though the answer calls for faith.

As we have noted repeatedly, Jesus is not telling us not to work or never to accumulate. In fact, the Apostle Paul later taught, "If anyone will not work, neither shall he eat" (2 Thess. 3:10). Also, the church is taught to "lay by in store" or "lay something aside" for future needs in the kingdom (1 Cor. 16:1-2).

As recorded in Matthew 6:25-34, Jesus does tell us not to "worry" about from where our food, clothing, or shelter will come. First of all, life consists of more than these simple necessities. Secondly, God provides abundantly for the necessities of lower forms of life, like the birds of the air and flowers of the field. Human beings are much more valuable, having eternal souls and being made in the image of God. Therefore, Jesus concludes God will take care of us also.

Further, worrying about such things does not change them. God's provision involves our working also, but we should never imagine by our work alone we obtain those things we need. Worry is an unhealthy degree of concern. Worry focuses the mind on one issue to the point all others are subordinated to it. If our worry is about physical provisions, then the spiritual component of life becomes subordinated to such physical concerns.

According to Jesus, the proper approach to work and money is getting the priority straight. "But seek first the kingdom of God and his righteousness, and all these things shall be added to you."

**Do Not Be Afraid To Ask God For Help**

A major part of the answer to our physical needs is spiritual in nature. Jesus said, "Ask and it will be given to you; seek, and you will find; knock, and it will be opened to you" (Matt. 7:7). The Lord undoubtedly was speaking more broadly than just physical provisions. He illustrated His point by demonstrating when earthly fathers are asked for food, they provide their children what is needful, and so will God (Matt. 7:9-11).

Rather than worrying or focusing too much of our energy on making money, we need to spend more time talking to God about our needs. Be confident and He will provide what we really need.

### Parables Related To Money, Possessions

Jesus was a Master Teacher. He took the universal interests of His students or disciples and used stories about every day experiences and work—especially concerns about money, investing, debt, wealth accumulation, poverty, property, wage structures, treasures, and capital investment—to teach about things they had not given much thought.

He demonstrated how to create a spiritual conversation and intense interest by starting a discussion on topics of great material interest. About twenty five percent of the Lord's parables involve money or material possessions in one way or the other. With those topics, He captured attention and assured His message would be memorable and of continuing interest to those who would read of His interchanges in centuries to come.

**Parable Of The Rich Fool—Luke 12:16-21**

Jesus tells this story when one of two brothers comes to the Lord asking Him to arbitrate a dispute over an inheritance. The Lord's primary response is, "Take heed and beware of covetousness, for one's life does not consist in the abundance of the things he possesses" (Luke 12:15).

To cement this message, He tells of a rich farmer whose fields yielded so much produce he did not have room to store it all. He decided to build larger barns and entrust his life or soul to the security of his physical wealth. In his folly, he said, "Soul, you have many goods laid up for many years; take your ease; eat, drink, and be merry."

God said to him, " 'Fool! This night your soul will be required of you; then whose will those things be which you have provided?'"

The **issue** is not necessarily whether you have **wealth**, but what role it plays in the **priorities** of your **life**.

Again, Jesus delivered His main point: "So is he who lays up treasure for himself, and is not rich toward God." In one brief story, the Lord teaches against greed, hoarding, not being rich toward God, and not trusting in God.

Jesus did not condemn the man for being rich, but for trusting in his riches. The story is powerful because such a man—and he represents every materialist—is shown to be silly, naïve, and sinful.

## Parables Using Money And Material Goods As The Backdrop

This group of parables utilizes human interest in money, wealth, wages, surprise windfalls, debts, and other such matters to teach important spiritual lessons, especially about the kingdom of heaven.

Learning occurs by associating new information with things already familiar. In other words, we learn by comparison and contrast. Few things are more familiar to us than monetary and material issues. So, Jesus used these as a backdrop for several parables.

Jesus' purpose in these parables was not particularly to evaluate or attack various aspects of the economic structures and procedures of Palestine. He simply used what was familiar to teach more valuable lessons.

Here are some examples of how Jesus used familiarity with monetary and material things to teach about spiritual matters. This list should not be considered exhaustive.

| Parable | Economic Illustration | Spiritual Application |
|---|---|---|
| Hidden Treasure Matt. 13:44 | Discovery of hidden treasure; man sells all he has to obtain it | How a person reacts when they unexpectedly discover the kingdom of heaven and its value |
| Pearl of Great Price Matt. 13:45-46 | How a man seeking something of economic value will sell all he has to obtain it | Shows how a person seeking kingdom of heaven will give up all he has to be a part of it |
| Unforgiving servant Matt. 18:23-35 | The burden of debt | Importance of forgiveness and how sinful it is to not forgive others when we've been forgiven our sins |
| Workers in the vineyard Matt. 20:1-16 | Hiring procedures and wage structures in first century | God's sovereignty and generosity in treating all men equally |
| Wicked vinedressers Matt. 21:33-46; Mark 12:1-12; Luke 20:9-19 | Leasing property | Israel's role, failures and evil attitudes relative to the kingdom of heaven...and their rejection of Messiah |

| Parable | Economic Illustration | Spiritual Application |
|---|---|---|
| Talents and Minas<br>Matt. 25:14-30; Luke 19:11-27 | Capital, investments, banking and interest accrual | Responsibility we have to use blessings/gifts God gives us wisely in the kingdom of heaven |
| Two debtors<br>Luke 7:41-43 | Money-lending, interest and debt cancellation | Link between God's forgiveness and our love and appreciation of Him |
| Tower builders<br>Luke 14:28-30 | Architectural planning, building and cost analysis | Importance of "counting the cost" before making spiritual decisions |
| Lost coin<br>Luke 15:8-10 | Human joy at finding lost money | Joy of angels over lost soul which is recovered |
| Prodigal son<br>Luke 15:11-32 | Wealth, dividing up an estate, irresponsible spending | Importance of repentance and a powerful picture of God's forgiveness |
| Unjust steward<br>Luke 16:1-12 | Bad financial management and dishonest debt reduction | Dishonest business people sometimes wiser than honest followers of Christ in using their resources in anticipation of final accounting |
| Pharisee and tax collector<br>Luke 18:9-14 | Tithing and taxes | Uselessness of fasting and tithing if done without humility before God |

## ➤ Questions ◄

1. Though giving materials gifts to God is a basis of worship, what is necessary for these gifts to be acceptable to God? _____
_____
_____
_____

2. Reconcile Jesus' statements in Matthew 6:2-4 and 5:14-16 about good deeds being seen by others. _____
_____
_____
_____
_____

3. Does Jesus' words concerning laying up treasures in heaven versus laying up treasures on earth forbid a Christian from saving and investing money? Explain. ____
_____
_____
_____
_____
_____

4.  What is mammon and how can a Christian be guilty of serving mammon? _____
    _____
    _____
    _____
    _____

5.  At what point does concern for material things become the worry which Jesus forbids?
    _____
    _____
    _____
    _____
    _____

6.  Describe the occasion on which Jesus told the parable of the rich fool (Luke 12:16-21).  _____
    _____
    _____
    _____
    _____

# MATERIALISM:
# A SPIRITLESS VIEW OF THE WORLD

As we explore the problem and sin called materialism, we will focus primarily on the excessive interest a majority of people have in making money, acquiring things and trying to define themselves by what they possess. Materialism involves more than these symptoms. It is an outlook on life leaving God out or making Him secondary to this material world. It casts man's spiritual nature into second place and his physical desires into first. This is a recipe for sin of every sort.

The Apostle Paul had what we call materialism in mind when he wrote to Timothy, "But those who desire to be rich fall into temptation and a snare, and into many foolish and harmful lusts which drown men in destruction and perdition. For the love of money is a root of all kinds of evil, for which some have strayed from the faith in their greediness, and pierced themselves through with many sorrows" (1 Tim. 6:9-10).

Notice some of the key words and phrases the apostle uses to describe this phenomenon. He mentions the "desire to be rich," "harmful lusts," "love of money," and "greediness." Elsewhere, the Bible uses the term "covetousness" to describe some aspects of this sin. It also is important to observe the apostle's warnings about the results of materialism. They include "destruction and perdition," "evil," "straying from the faith," and "piercing themselves through with many sorrows." Materialism makes promises it cannot keep and delivers unimaginable sorrows in this life—even if we set aside for the moment the eternal consequences.

Materialism menaces modern families. It lurks just below the surface of daily life. Most people are vaguely aware of its existence, but ignorant of its actual potential. It functions like cancer, first making a small appearance, but then metastasizing.

The cancer comparison serves well in defining materialism. Ask 100 people to define the term. There may be 100 variant answers. This is because materialism is so immense in scope. Like the array of cancers attacking the human bodies, materialism is a

> But those who **desire** to be **rich** fall into temptation and **a snare**, and into many foolish and harmful lusts which **drown** men in **destruction** and perdition. For the **love** of **money** is a root of all kinds of **evil**...
> (1 Timothy 6:9-10)

multi-faceted coalition of spiritual diseases consuming human souls and casting them into the abyss of eternal hell.

"Vast numbers of us have been seduced into believing that having more wealth and material possessions is essential to a good life. We have swallowed the idea that, to be well, one first must be well off. And many of us, consciously or unconsciously, have learned to evaluate our own wellbeing and accomplishment not by looking inward at our spirit or integrity, but by looking outward at what we have and what we can buy," writes Tim Kasser, associate professor of psychology at Knox College (Kasser, 2002).

Yet most families do not see the tentacles of materialism enveloping their hearts. Deceived, more see materialism as the answer to life's dilemmas, rather than the cause of those problems and afflictions. Popular culture and especially the culture of the business world suggest selfishness and materialism are not moral problems, but the keys to success.

While people are getting more and more, evidence all around suggests life has not become better as a result of increased income and possessions.

Writer Randy Alcorn has coined the term "affluenza" to describe materialism as it afflicts modern American life. "Affluenza is a strange malady that affects the children of well-to-do parents. Though having everything money can buy, the children show all the symptoms of abject poverty—depression, anxiety, loss of meaning, and despair for the future. Affluenza accounts for an escape into alcohol, drugs, shoplifting, and suicide among children of the wealthy. It is most often found where parents are absent from the house and try to buy their children's love" (Alcorn, 2003).

The most visible manifestations of materialism—conspicuous consumption, gross selfishness, insatiable cravings for more and better, and frantic lifestyles—are oft-addressed issues in the secular press and the pulpit.

The root of materialism lies in a philosophy sweeping Europe and now besieges America. Often associated with humanism and secularization, this life rationale begins with the elimination of God and proceeds to eradicate the spiritual element from human life. At its logical conclusion, there is nothing but the material world.

Randy Alcorn writes, "Materialism will inevitably produce the kind of society increasingly evident in America—a society of individualism, where people live parallel lives, not meaningfully intersecting with others. A society where independence is the only absolute, where self-interest is the only creed, where convenience and expediency and profitability are the only values. A society where people know the price of everything, but the value of nothing—where people have a great deal to live on, but very little to live for" (Alcorn, 2003).

While we may be focusing on excessive consumption and teenagers' demands to have the latest jeans, shoes and "looks," materialism has some more deadly legacies. These include:
• Rejection of reason and objective truth.
• Rejection of objective morality.
• Rejection of personal responsibility.

This makes the assault of materialism on the home all the more pernicious. We can become so affected by materialism that we cannot even recognize it. When objective truth and morality (as defined in God's word) are set aside, who will take personal responsibility and admit, "I'm materialistic"?  The typical person, even the average Christian, does not seem to know materialism when he sees it—at least in his own life. Is materialism having a lot of stuff? Is it an attitude? Do you have to be rich to be materialistic, or can poor people be such? For the majority, materialism is a problem or sin of someone else.

We tend to ignore materialism for the very reason we are materialistic. To know we are materialistic requires us to examine the spiritual component of our lives, where our heart is focused. Materialism denies the importance or existence of such a spiritual factor.

### Evidence Of Materialism All Around Us

The evidence of materialism's presence is all around us, though it often is not recognized. Below are just a few examples of materialism's impact in 21st Century culture and American life.

- Growth of gambling: There is a rise in the number of people who are problematic gamblers.  This rise includes those who are teenagers.
- Our greedy state governments enthusiastically switched from policing the "numbers rackets" to operating them as state lotteries.
- Upsurge in bankruptcies: Millions of Americans file for bankruptcy each year, including a fair number of Christians. Misuse of credit and greedy materialism causes many of these bankruptcies.
- Divorce crisis: When both spouses focus primarily on making money, there is little time to give to one another. Few marriages can survive inattention.
- Epidemic of sleep disorders afftection Americans.  Financial stress is a leading contributor to loss of sleep.
- Pitiful giving patterns: While it is impossible to accurately document what Christians give in their Lord's Day offerings, Internal Revenue Service analysis shows that of Americans who itemize their deductions, the average American gives less than three percent to church and charity combined. The Barna Group confirms this by polling done among professed Christians.
- Creation of a new class of orphans: Millions of "latchkey" children come home from school every day to empty homes. Some parents shuffle their children off to day care centers, where they live life much like orphans because both parents are so busy working to provide the family the "things" they want.
- Murder of unborn babies: Yes, abortion is mostly a fruit of materialism. Many view a baby  as an inconvenience, an economic hardship, an impediment to job advancement, or a lifestyle spoiler.

Writer Randy Alcorn has coined the term **"affluenza"** to describe **materialism** as it **afflicts** modern American **life**.

- Euthanasia: A growing number have the disposition to help older people die, once their ability to care for themselves is gone. When they are just an economic hardship, they are viewed as expendable.
- Pandemic of depression and other unaccounted for illnesses: Studies show the more materialistic people are the more anxiety, stress, and depression they suffer. This general unhappiness causes a host of health problems, ranging from sleeplessness to headaches, backaches, sore muscles and sore throats.
- Hectic hysteria: Despite continually multiplying the number of time and labor saving devices, many Americans constantly talk about their frantic lives.
- Social isolation: More and more people either live alone or as families live in isolation from neighbors and their community. Interpersonal relationships decline as people become more absorbed in television, computers, and the like. Close relationships are one foundation of psychological health and high quality of life. Conversely, isolation weakens the fibers binding couples, friends, families and communities. We might add—churches.
- Upsurge in compulsive buying: Inability to control one's appetite for buying things has become the newest addiction to require treatment in the 21st Century. Intense impulses drive many to purchase things even when individuals know they are not needed.
- The Disneyland gospel: This is the health and wealth doctrine popularized by TV evangelists like Jim Bakker, Oral Roberts, Benny Hinn and Kenneth and Gloria Copeland. It argues God wants us all to be physically rich. Wealth is equated with spirituality. Taken to its logical conclusion, if a person is poor or only of moderate means, he or she must be spiritually weak or sinful.

The evidence of materialism's existence and impact is overwhelming. Now, we need to focus on God's answers for this pervasive human problem.

### Jesus On Materialism

The absolute foolishness of focusing only on the material part of life was Jesus' point when He told the parable of the rich fool. "The ground of a certain rich man yielded plentifully. And he thought within himself, saying, 'What shall I do, since I have no room to store my crops?' So he said, ' I will do this: I will pull down my barns and build greater, and there I will store all my crops and my goods. And I will say to my soul, Soul, you have many goods laid up for many years, take your ease; eat drink, and be merry.' But God said to him, 'Fool! This night your soul will be required of you; then whose will those things be which you have provided?'" (Luke 12:16-20).

This parable clearly describes a materialist. All the rich man's confidence and sense of security was invested in what he owned. He had more than he could use, yet selfishly failed to consider those less fortunate. He only thought of his own ease and pleasure. God called this man a fool, for he gave no consideration to what would become of his soul when material life ended.

The Lord demonstrated the end of such fools also when He told of the rich man and Lazarus (Luke 16:19-31). This rich man found his material blessings did not follow him beyond the grave. In torment, he agonized for just a drop of water and desired to send word to warn family members still living. It is worth noting Jesus did not accuse this rich man of getting his wealth by stealing or other sinful means. He simply made them the primary focus of his life.

In His Sermon on the Mount, Jesus made clear materialistic attitudes and behavior are incompatible with discipleship and citizenship in the kingdom of heaven. "Do not lay up for yourselves treasures on earth, where moth and rust destroy and where thieves break in and steal; but lay up for yourselves treasures in heaven, where neither moth nor rust destroys and where thieves do not break in and steal. For where your treasure is, there your heart will be also" (Matt.6:19-21). The Lord went to the "heart" of the issue. What a person places as the priority or treasure of their life defines who and what they are. One is a materialist and a lover of this world if money and physical things are their priority. One is a disciple of Jesus and a lover of God if the spiritual and the kingdom of God have priority in their thinking and behavior.

Can we be a little bit materialistic and also be spiritual? Jesus answers emphatically, "No one can serve two masters; for either he will hate the one and love the other, or else he will be loyal to the one and despise the other. You cannot serve God and mammon" (Matt. 6:24). Jesus' exchange with a rich young man who came to learn what he needed to do to obtain eternal life illustrates this point. Jesus told him to keep God's commandments. The young man replied he had done so since his youth. So, the Lord told him to sell all he had and give it to the poor. The young man could not bring himself to do this and left sorrowfully (Matt. 19:16-22). Jesus knew the young man had divided loyalties. He wanted to be a materialist and inherit eternal life. Jesus nixed the idea.

Yet the material heart retorts, "But I have to make a living!" Jesus answers again, "Therefore I say to you, do not worry about your life, what you will eat or what you will drink; nor about your body, what you will put on. Is not life more than food, and the body more than clothing?" (Matt.6:25). One of the symptoms of a materialistic heart is worry or anxiety. It is because the materialist sees himself as self-dependent.

Jesus proceeded to attack the mythology of self-dependence by pointing to the natural world and God's superintending providence. "Look at the birds of the air," He said, "for they neither sow nor reap nor gather into barns; yet your heavenly Father feeds them. Are you not of much more value than they? Which of you by worrying can add one cubit to his stature? So why do you worry about clothing? Consider the lilies of the field, how they grow: they neither toil nor spin; and yet I say to you that even Solomon in all his glory was not arrayed like one of these. Now if God so clothes the grass of the field, which today is, and tomorrow is thrown into the oven, will He not much more clothe you, O you of little faith?" (Matt.6:26-30).

Materialism, remember, seeks to make the material world all there is and to leave God out of the equation. This is the myth of materialism. Jesus demonstrated the fallacy of the myth by focusing on God's provision for lesser forms of life than human beings. Those grasses and animals are provided for in superb ways without the anxiety and energies the materialist expends. If God does this for soul-less birds and flowers, what will He do for those created in His own image?

### Important To Keep Spiritual Element In The First Place

Jesus urged His disciples to focus primarily on the spiritual aspect of life, putting God's kingdom, Christ's rule, and obedience to the divine pattern at the center of life. The Lord said God would provide for our material and physical needs in due course. "But seek first the kingdom of God and His righteousness, and all these things will be added to you. Therefore, do not worry about tomorrow, for tomorrow will worry about its own things. Sufficient for the day is its own trouble" (Matt.6:33-34). The Lord's conclusion is remarkably similar to Solomon's conclusion in Eccl. 12:13, "Let us hear the conclusion of the whole matter: Fear God and keep His commandments, for this is man's all" (NKJV).

Spirituality does not preclude thought and work designed to provide for ourselves materially. The man who will not work to provide for his family is deemed "worse than an infidel" (1 Tim. 5:8). Jesus rebuked any effort to justify such failure with some sort of fake spirituality. "All too well you reject the commandment of God, that you may keep your tradition. For Moses said, 'Honor your father and your mother'; and 'He who curses father or mother, let him be put to death.' But you say, 'If a man says to his father or mother, "Whatever profit you might have received from me is Corban"—'(that is, a gift to God), then you no longer let him do anything for his father or mother, making the word of God of no effect through your tradition which you have handed down. And many such things you do" (Mark 7:9-13).

The number of neglected parents in America suggests the materialism underlying such spiritual tomfoolery remains quite alive in the 21st Century.

The example of the Lord is instructive. If ever a man might be justified in neglecting His family, it would be the impoverished Lord, the day all His work and mission culminated in His death for our sins. Despite the agony of scourging and crucifixion, and regardless of the emotional and spiritual wretchedness He bore in shouldering the sins of mankind, He arranged from the cross for the care of His mother (John 19:25-27).

### Cited

Kasser, T. (2002). *The high price of materialism*. (pp. ix-x). Cambridge, MA. and London: A Bradford Book, the MIT Press.

Alcorn, R. (2003). *Money, possessions, and eternity*. (Revised Edition ed., p. 382). Wheaton, IL: Tyndale House Publishers.

Alcorn, R. (2003). *Money, possessions, and eternity*. (Revised Edition ed., p. 17). Wheaton, IL: Tyndale House Publishers.

### ➢ Questions ◄

1. Define materialism. _____
_____
_____
_____

2. What are some dangers resulting from materialism? _____
_____
_____
_____
_____
_____

3. Why is materialism deceptive? _____
_____
_____
_____
_____
_____

4.  Based upon the Parable of the Rich Fool and the story of the Rich Man and Lazarus, how do we know materialism not defined by how much one possesses? In these two cases, how is materialism defined? _____

    _____

    _____

    _____

    _____

5.  From Jesus' Sermon on the Mount (Matt. 6:19-34), list some ways a disciple of Christ can prevent materialism. _____

    _____

    _____

    _____

# MATERIALISM:
# ITS PROMISES BELIED BY ITS RESULTS

One of the allures of materialism is its promise of freedom. As many find out too late, it actually diminishes freedom. Husbands working long hours to pay huge debts for "toys" find there is no time left to use or enjoy them. Wives join the workforce, commit to paying the same debts, and find the same results. Both come home from work exhausted, but still facing the chores of keeping up the home. Where is the freedom?

The promise of prosperity is a less stressful and more relaxed life. The boat and recreational vehicles and mountain cabin are supposed to usher in "the life." Instead, they create a demanding rat race to meet the payments, pay for maintenance, insurance, and more taxes.

Many parents justify their materialistic quests as being "for their children." What their children need is time and teaching from their parents. Sadly, many parents raise kids so materialistic they are brats when very young, hoodlums in their teen years, and so busy making money themselves when they become adults they have no interest in or time for their now aging parents.

### The Failed Promises Of Materialism Are Not Really News

Solomon discovered money and possessions do not bring happiness centuries ago. God inspired him to write his discoveries in Ecclesiastes, part of the wisdom literature of the Old Testament.

The third king of Israel is a worthwhile case study in the vanity (uselessness) of a materialistic pursuit of happiness and meaning in life. Solomon found every earthly pursuit, if the spiritual guidance of the Almighty is lacking, brings no real reward. For most of us, consideration of what life would be like if we were billionaires and able to demand anything we wanted is mere speculation. Solomon had the wealth and kingly governmental power to explore every materialistic avenue to its extremity.

Many **parents raise kids** so materialistic they are **brats** when very **young**, **hoodlums** in their **teens**, and so busy **making money** for themselves when they become **adults** they have no interest in or time for their now aging parents.

Here are the things with which he experimented. Compare them to materialistic pursuits today.

- Mirth, pleasure, and laughter (2:1-2)
- Fine dining (2:3)
- Beautiful houses with pools, gardens, orchards, and vineyards (2:4-5)
- Numerous servants to do work for him (2:7)
- Cattle and livestock ranches—businesses producing income (2:7)
- Bank accounts of silver and gold (2:8)
- Vast stores of valuable "collectibles" (2:8)
- Musical entertainment (2:8)
- Power, position, and prestige (2:9)

Solomon said, "Whatever my eyes desired I did not keep from them. I did not withhold my heart from any pleasure...Then I looked on all the works that my hands had done and on the labor in which I had toiled; and indeed all was vanity and grasping at the wind" (2:10-11).

Ever tried to "grasp the wind"? It is impossible and so is finding freedom, security, happiness and sense of wellbeing in materialistic pursuits. Solomon said he did not refrain from any effort to find pleasure—but still found it all vanity. In addition to all the things mentioned in Ecclesiastes, we know Solomon also surrounded himself with 700 wives and 300 concubines. He had beautiful women on his arms, and abundant sexual pleasures were his to enjoy. Instead of serving him well, they drew him away from God and into a materialistic religious experience. He built temples and worshipped gods of wood, stone and metal (1 Kings 11:1-8).

Solomon found possessions do not deliver happiness. Rather, they create new and difficult problems:

- "When goods increase, they increase who eat them; so what profit have the owners except to see them with their eyes?" (Eccl. 5:11). He refers to all the servants he had to feed, clothe, and shelter to maintain and manage his possessions. The modern equivalent might be accountants, tax consultants, investment advisors, repairmen and other hired help.
- "The sleep of a laboring man is sweet, whether he eats little or much; but the abundance of the rich will not permit him to sleep" (Eccl. 5:12).
- "Then I hated all my labor in which I had toiled under the sun, because I must leave it to the man who will come after me. And who knows whether he will be wise or a fool?" (Eccl. 2:18-19) The rich man has to worry about whether his wealth will bless or ruin his children.

"...I did not **withhold** my heart from any **pleasure**...
...indeed **all** was vanity and **grasping** at the **wind**" (Ecclesiastes 2:10-11).

## Materialism Functions Like Addiction

The addict to alcohol, drugs, pornography or gambling discovers rather quickly it takes more and more of the substance or habit to satisfy the craving or make life seem tolerable. The pursuit of material things operates exactly the same.

Most of us have experienced the truth of this. When we were young and just starting out in life, we thought a nice little tract house and a decent used car would make us happy. It did, briefly. Then, when we saw others with bigger and better houses and cars, we thought we would be happier if we could get those things, too.

What happened? Our imagined baseline of happiness moved. Once we managed to achieve the new baseline, it moved again.

Again, this is not some new discovery. Solomon wrote nearly 3,000 years ago, "Yet there is no end to his labors, nor is his eye satisfied with riches" (Eccl. 4:8). Again, "He who loves silver will not be satisfied with silver; nor he who loves abundance, with increase. This also is vanity" (Eccl. 5:10).

## The Role Of Television

Television may be the single greatest purveyor of materialism. From programming to advertising, most of what appears on TV is predominantly materialistic. Movies, talk shows, situation comedies, soap operas, and weekly dramas all emphasize and glamorize the carnal and the worldly. Even the news is mostly devoid of any focus on the spiritual.

Television programming presents drinking, gambling, and sexual deviancy as "normal." There are even shows where women try to "sell" themselves for marriage to a millionaire. Others emphasize the importance of an external "make-over" to feel good or have a good self-image. Nice cars, beautiful houses, manicured lawns, leisure time around the pool, and prestigious jobs are the backdrop to many shows.

Then comes the advertising, sometimes overtly and other times covertly, selling dissatisfaction with everything about life and touting all sorts of promises if you just buy this product.

No wonder many parents have a bunch of little whiners and beggars on their hands, always demanding this new toy or brand of new clothing. Many of these parents, totally materialistic in their thinking, assume they have to fulfill these demands or their children will hate them, grow up deprived, warped, and ruined.

The result, however, in spite of closets bursting with unused clothing and rooms so full of toys one cannot walk about, is a generation of some of the brattiest children the world has ever produced.

## Materialism Has Invaded The Church

It is an oft-repeated truism—whatever troubles the world and denominationalism will one day trouble the Lord's church. This is certainly true regarding carnality and materialism.

Awe-inspiring buildings, performance and entertainment in the place of true worship, the social, health, and wealth gospels, and most recently the super Walmart-style mega-churches with their latte bars, gymnasiums, finance seminars, and politically correct, all-inclusive and inoffensive messages simply ooze the message of materialism.

In his book *Hot Tube Religion*, J.I. Packer has called this "hot tub religion" and went on to say, "...it struck me that the hot tub is the perfect symbol of the modern route of religion. The hot tub experience is sensuous, relaxing, floppy, laid-back; not in any way demanding, whether intellectually or otherwise...Many today want Christianity to be like that, and labor to make it so. The ultimate step, of course, would be to clear church auditoriums of seats and install hot tubs in their place; then there would never be any attendance problems" (Packer, 1987).

He continued, "Symptoms of hot tub religion today include a skyrocketing divorce and re-marriage rate among Christians; widespread indulgence of sexual aberrations; an overheated supernaturalism that seeks signs, wonders, visions, prophecies and miracles; constant soothing syrup from electronic preachers and the liberal pulpit; anti-intellectual sentimentalism and emotional 'highs' deliberately cultivated, the Christian equivalent of cannabis and coca; and an easy, thoughtless acceptance of luxury in everyday living" (Packer, 1987).

Packer's premises pinpoint the problems and peculiarities of carnality and materialism in the denominational church. Look carefully at the Lord's church. What is often defined as liberalism and one can see seeds, sprouts and symptoms of the very same things.

### Materialism Changes How We Look At People

When money and things rule our thinking, they also define how we measure and value other people. Many in business today look at people merely as "consumers," economic units buying products and creating profit. Products are marketed and advertised to consumers without regard to the fact consumers may become addicted, lose their livelihoods, become sick, obese, and diseased—or even die.

A materialist judges the value and importance of people on such criteria as their job, position, wealth, looks or secular level of education.

Materialist judge others based on their power, their ability to help us materially or the honors their association brings, rather than assessing people on the basis of spiritual factors, like their love, goodness, kindness, self-control, and faithfulness.

This is not only singularly wrong; it also undermines the very purpose of our lives and the mission of the Lord's church. James put it this way, "My brethren, do not hold the faith of our Lord Jesus Christ, the Lord of glory, with partiality. For if there should come into your assembly a man with gold rings, in fine apparel, and there should also come in a poor man in filthy clothes, and you pay attention to the one wearing the fine clothes and say to him, 'You sit here in a good place,' and say to the poor man, 'You stand there,' or 'Sit here at my footstool,' have you not shown partiality among yourselves, and become judges with evil thoughts?" (James 2:1-4) Then, in verse 9 he declares, "but if you show partiality you commit sin."

We need to be lights in a dark world and salt in an unsavory society (Matt. 5:13-16). Our mission as the church of Christ is to "Go into all the world and preach the gospel to every creature" (Mark 16:15) and to "make disciples of all the nations" (Matt. 28:19). All of this is impossible when we measure men carnally, rather than spiritually.

The cross of Christ is evidence of God's love for all (John 3:16). The Lord is "longsuffering toward us, not willing that any should perish but that all should come to repentance" (2 Peter 3:9). He values the souls of all men and shows no partiality with regard to a man's possessions, earthly position or power.

If the missionary zeal of the Lord's church is today stymied, could it be because materialistic value systems have devalued the souls of sinners in our eyes and left us willing to evangelize only those we deem similar to ourselves?

### Families Ignore Bible Warnings At Own Peril

The Bible has a number of illustrations of rich men who pleased God. Among these were Job, Abraham, David, Solomon (for a time), and Joseph of Arimathea. The successful mixing of wealth and spirituality is the exception, not the rule. Jesus made this clear when He said, "Assuredly I say to you that it is hard for a rich man to enter the kingdom of heaven. And again I say to you, it is easier for a camel to go through the eye of a needle than for a rich man to enter the kingdom of God" (Matt.19:23-24). Being amazed, his disciples asked who would be able to enter the kingdom. Jesus' answer was, "With men this is impossible, but with God all things are possible" (Matt. 19:26). Only through careful obedience to the principles of God's word can anyone, particularly the rich, enter God's kingdom. Just remember, when it comes to spiritual things, it is the rich who are disadvantaged.

The Apostle Paul reiterated and expanded upon the Lord's teaching when he wrote, "And having food and clothing, with these we shall be content. But those who desire to be rich fall into temptation and a snare, and into many foolish and harmful lusts, which drown men in destruction and perdition. For the love of money is the root of all kinds of evil, for which some have strayed from the faith in their greediness, and pierced themselves through with many sorrows" (1 Tim.6:8-10).

While the rich have great difficulty entering God's kingdom, let us recognize the poor and the merely comfortable face disaster also if their hearts are set on the "desire to be rich." Poor people can be every bit as materialistic as rich ones.

The apostle urged contentment with what we have, whether little or much. In writing to the Philippians, he said, "I have learned in whatever state I am to be content. I know how to be abased, and I know how to abound. Everywhere and in all things I have learned both to be full and to be hungry, both to abound and to suffer need" (4:11-12).

Again, he did not say being rich was the problem. He said the "desire" to be rich is what propels people into all sorts of temptations and traps. This desire evolves into foolish and harmful lusts leading men to destruction.

Money is not the problem. The "love of money" is the sub-surface root of all kinds of evil. We looked at some of those evils in our last lesson. Greed leads men to forsake their faith and then suffer all sorts of sorrows as materialism serves up the opposite of every promise it makes.

### A Closer Look At Greed

Greed is another term that helps us understand materialism. Greed has two elements:
• Possessiveness: Our attitude regarding what we already possess.
• Covetousness: An ungodly desire for what we don't possess.

The answer is self-denial, particularly denial of the flesh to satisfy every carnal urging. Remember Jesus' words. "If anyone desires to come after Me, let him deny himself, and take up his cross daily, and follow Me" (Luke 9:23). John wrote, "Do not love the world or the things in the world. If anyone loves the world, the love of the Father is not in him. For all that is in the world—the lust of the flesh, the lust of the eyes, and the pride of life—is not of the Father but is of the world" (1 John 2:15-16).

### So, How Do We Avoid The Trap Of Materialism?

Jesus told us to seek the kingdom of heaven first and our material needs will be met. Few people have enough faith in God's promise to trust this approach to life. Others misunderstand it and they fail to work. The Apostle Paul said if a man will not work, he should not eat, and brethren should not give him a handout (2 Thess. 3:6-14).

Jesus was not teaching us to sit and wait for manna from heaven, but to make the focus, the priority, and the mission of our lives serving God and doing His will. This is spiritual living.

Many seem to think if they spend their lives in worship, teaching others, helping the needy, comforting the sick, and being diligent to mature into a person approved by God they will not have any time or money for physical necessities. They are wrong. Jesus said so.

When one focuses their heart on God's kingdom and righteousness, it eliminates several things that can strip a man of wealth and happiness. These include covetousness, selfishness, and greed. Many Christians have seen their prosperity soar and their ability to meet their family's needs surpassed so he has extra with which to help others. When a man does what he knows is right, he feels good about it and about himself. The result is contentment and happiness.

As we noted, the Apostle Paul said, a man who is doing right can be content and happy whether he has much or little.

Ultimately, what every person in this world craves is contentment and happiness. Materialism promises such, but the life focused in Christ produces the wellbeing we all desire.

In his letter to the church at Rome, the Apostle Paul contrasted two approaches to life. One was a "walk according to the flesh." The other walk was "according to the Spirit." He said, "For those who live according to the flesh set their minds on the things of the flesh, but those who live according to the Spirit, the things of the Spirit. For to be carnally minded is death, but to be spiritually minded is life and peace" (8:1-6). The apostle's point in this passage is broader than our application here, but certainly includes our point.

When all this is summarized, the emphasis is on living a God-directed life. This is what spirituality is all about.

When we fail to inculcate the spiritual into the lives of our families, we rob our children and ourselves of the best of God's gifts, and we bring upon ourselves the curses of disobedience. We have clearly demonstrated materialism is disobedience. It is sin.

The challenge today is to teach our children about money and possessions. The oft-quoted proverb is never truer than in this context. "Train up a child in the way he should go, and when he is old he will not depart from it" (Prov. 22:6). Teach your children to give and show them "it is more blessed to give than to receive" (Acts 20:35).

Randy Alcorn has suggested a good teaching experience for children. "Try taking them to a junkyard or a dump. It can actually be a great family event. Show them all the piles of 'treasures' that were formerly Christmas and birthday presents. Point out things that cost hundreds of dollars, that children quarreled about, friendships were lost over, honesty sacrificed for, and marriages broken up over. Show them the miscellaneous arms and legs and remnants of battered dolls, rusted robots, and electronic gadgets that now lie useless after their brief life span. Point out to them that most of what your family owns will one day be in a junkyard like this. Read 2 Peter 3:10-14, which tells us everything will be consumed by fire. Then ask this telling question, 'When all that we owned lies abandoned, broken, and useless, what will we have done that will last for eternity?'" (Alcorn, 2003).

## Am I Materialistic?

None of us totally escape the traps of materialism. So, the question, "Am I materialistic?" is like the question, "Am I a sinner?" If by either question we mean do I ever act in accordance with fleshly desires or do I ever sin, the answer to both questions is "yes."

If the questions pertain to whether my general habit of life is to be a materialist or a sinner, a closer self-examination is needed.

If one is seriously interested in answering this question, they need to look at two things: their checkbook and their daily planner or calendar. They need to look carefully at what they spend their money on and how they spend their time. Once they have a good mental picture of their habits, they can compare them to what the Lord and His spokesmen set as spiritual living. Remember the Lord said, "Blessed are those who hunger and thirst for righteousness, for they shall be filled" (Matt. 5:6). For what do we hunger and thirst?

## Cited

Packer, J.I. (1987). *Hot Tub Religion*. Wheaton, IL.: Tyndale House Publishers.

Alcorn, R. (2003). Money, possessions, and eternity. Wheaton, IL.: Tyndale House Publishers.

## ➤ Questions ◄

1. List some things promised by materialism. _____
_____
_____
_____
_____

2. Why was Solomon unable to find happiness from his possessions? _____
_____
_____
_____
_____
_____

3.  Describe the influence of televion on people in regards to materialism. Why does television have such an influence? _____
_____
_____
_____
_____
_____

4.  Discuss the effects of materialism on the Lord's church today. _____
_____
_____
_____
_____

5.  Regarding materialism, what are some warnings families seem to ignore?   _____
_____
_____
_____
_____
_____
_____

6.  How can one avoid the trap of materialism?   _____
_____
_____
_____
_____

# DANGERS OF DEBT

It is the American way. Most folks live in mortgaged houses, filled with furniture bought on installment plans, driving bank-financed cars run on gasoline purchased by credit-card to take vacations on a home equity line of credit. It seems a great life as long as the minimum payments can be made—and if nothing unforeseen happens to health or employment.

The flip side of the coin is bankruptcy—seeking a legal escape from a moral responsibility when the unforeseen happens, and we cannot pay what we promised. In 2005, more than 2 million households filed bankruptcy in this country, about one in every 60 households.

The Bible does not outright condemn all indebtedness, but it raises red flags about the practice. It does warn against and condemn many of the attitudes and disciplinary failures prompting many people to buy what they cannot afford.

### Attendant Problems To Debt

It also is reported financial pressures due to debts are a significant factor in 50 percent of divorces in this country. The average American family devotes 25 percent of its income to addressing outstanding debt. The IRS calculates the average tax filer spends 10 times more on debt interest than on charitable causes, which would include church contributions.

In 2007-2008, the stock market was very volatile. Housing prices slumped, new construction plummeted, and concerns rose about restricted credit affecting business profitability around the globe. What is the reported cause of all this? Most people blamed the lending practices letting people borrow money they could not really afford to repay and at escalating rates making repayment nearly impossible.

If you have ever been caught up in the downside of debt, you know the "dream" can become an absolute nightmare. If you have

The **Bible** does not outright condemn all **indebtedness**, but it raises **red flags** about the practice.

borrowed to replace a worn out car before paying off the exhausted auto, you know what they mean when they say you are "upside down."

If you have gone to one of the "pay-day lenders" and borrowed money for a couple of weeks, you may have discovered the meaning of the word "usury" and why it is evil. Many of these loans have effective annual rates as high as 400%. Hooked into a series of such loans, some people are virtually trapped for life.

### Warnings About Debt In The Bible

It is an over-statement to say the Bible condemns all debt, but it certainly is true God's word signals warnings about debt. In the wisdom literature of the Old Testament, we learn, "The rich rules over the poor, and the borrower is servant to the lender" (Proverbs 22:7). Some translations say, "is slave to the lender."

When one has agreed to debt, there is real sense in which one loses freedom. Promises and obligations made to others limits how one decides to use their time and money. If a person finds he cannot repay his debt, what he does possess can be taken.

The Bible sets the concept of good stewardship forth or prudently using the blessings which God supplies. Biblical stewardship applies to much more than finances, but certainly includes such. Consider Jesus words in Luke 16:10, "He who is faithful in what is least is faithful also in much; and he who is unjust in what is least is unjust also in much." Many debt problems are case studies in poor stewardship.

### Is All Debt Prohibited By Scripture?

It has become increasingly popular among a handful of denominational writers to allege all debt is sinful or contrary to God's will. The primary passage cited as a proof text is Romans 13:8, which reads, "Owe no one anything except to love one another, for he who loves another has fulfilled the law." This seems to be a case of pulling a text out of its context. The apostle appears to be dealing with Christians who thought they did not have to pay taxes or other bills because they were not of this world. Paul corrects this view and tells them to pay whomever they owe, including the government.

The Old Law set limitations about how long a person's land inheritance could be retained as collateral for a loan, as well as limitations on the length of servitude due to debt. While these issues, tied to Sabbath years and the year of Jubilee, may have had social value, their greater importance was tied to the land and nation promises made to Abraham and necessary to bringing the Christ into the world (Leviticus 25).

There were restrictions on making loans to poor brethren in the covenant nation, pressing the principle of love would willingly help a fellow Israelite without expectation of making a profit on his misfortune. None of this was designed to address borrowing for luxuries or investment.

Some make modern applications of the old debt relief codes of the Law of Moses without consideration of their context. One example is justification of bankruptcy or just walking away from one's debts. No New Testament passage justifies not keeping one's promise to repay a debt.

### Does This Mean All Indebtedness Is Acceptable?

Much of what we learn in the Bible concerning unacceptable debt has more to do with the sinful attitudes than debt itself. Greediness, lack of patience, sparse confidence in God's provisions, and a growing selfishness and lack of self-discipline accounts for the billions of dollars of debts most Americans now struggle to pay back.

The Apostle Paul wrote in Philippians 4:11, "Not that I speak in regard to need, for I have learned in whatever state I am, to be content." This is a concept virtually foreign to American minds. The advertising and entertainment industries have fueled an already raging level of popular discontent and craving for more and more...now!

The banking and lending industry has tapped into this greediness and made money easily available, though the average credit card interest rate is more than 18 percent. People assume they will have the job and income next month they have today and plunk down the plastic card. They fail to consider the warning in James 4:13-14, "Come now, you who say, 'Today or tomorrow we will go to such and such a city, spend a year there, buy and sell, and make a profit'; whereas you do not know what will happen tomorrow. For what is your life? It is even a vapor that appears for a little time and then vanishes away."

Ignoring this warning and seemingly unconcerned whether their families or their creditors get stuck with the debt should circumstances change, Americans have accumulated an average credit card debt of over $8,600. This does not include home mortgages, car loans, and other credit.

Many Christians are part of these statistics.

### Saving Versus Borrowing
### Is An Oft-Ignored Biblical Principle

It may seem a radical concept in the 21st Century, but the Bible promotes the concept of saving rather than continually borrowing. This is necessarily implied in the Apostle Paul's directive in Ephesians 4:28, "Let him who stole steal no longer, but rather let him labor, working with his hands what is good, that he may have something to give him who has need." If a person spends all he has, he will not have any to share. If he borrows against future earnings until all present and future assets are "tied up," he has the same problem.

The New Testament directive concerning funding the Lord's church contains the same idea. Paul wrote, "On the first day of the week let each one of you lay something aside, storing up as he may

> ...the **Bible** promotes the concept of **saving** rather than continually **borrowing**.

prosper, that there be no collections when I come" (1 Corinthians 16:2). This storing up or "laying by in store" suggests at least short term saving so that future needs can be met with ready resources. As one writer has pointed out somewhat humorously, there were no tabernacle bonds sold in the wilderness and Solomon did not finance construction of the great house of worship in Jerusalem on borrowed money.

### Churches And Debt

While borrowing to buy or build a church building may be more prudent than constant renting of a facility, churches need to be very careful about credit.

Interestingly, the lending world often views churches as poor credit risks. Financial instruments, known in the trade as "junk bonds," finance many buildings. Lenders have often been risk adverse because many churches historically failed to repay what they borrowed. Numbers of attendees plummet, churches divide, or other unexpected things happened and suddenly the ability to repay the debt is gone. How sad some churches would be viewed as poor risks in regard to repaying debts.

Denominations continue to build larger and larger buildings and complexes. There always is the temptation to keep up. Brethren should be aware borrowing for unnecessarily large or ornate buildings strips the church of resources to support the preaching of the gospel and provide for needy saints. Even if an error is acknowledged and repented of—the consequences may remain for another 25 or 30 years.

### Some Dangers In Debt You May Not Have Considered

Debt raises the potential you may become a thief and a liar! Many people do not seem to view reneging on a debt to a bank or credit card company in this way. If you borrowed money from a friend with a promise to repay and did not, are you not guilty of lying or stealing from him? Do your good intentions (the fact you planned to repay him when you borrowed and promised to repay) restore what your friend has lost? Who is defrauded, cheated, and hurt when you miscalculate your ability to repay and cannot fulfill your promise? Now, think of the spiritual impact you will have. How likely are you to convince your friend to become a Christian after you have defrauded him? The case is not any different if the lender is a bank instead of a friend.

Easy credit fuels materialism and a heavy focus on this world instead of spiritual things. Worldly people do not believe in delayed gratification. Real Christians are patient. For example, they wait to engage in sex until they are properly married. They do not let impulses lead them to lie or steal to gain something.

**Debt** raises the **potential** you may become a **thief** and a **liar**!

They recognize "this world is not my home" and ultimate gratification will be in heaven. This attitude establishes a whole different approach to earthly life.

Debt burdens can lead us to rob our families of what they need—our time. Time and money are, in reality, merely ways we measure our lives. When we owe tremendous financial debts, we must give greater and greater parts of ourselves to pay for those borrowings. This means less and less of ourselves we can invest in bringing our children up in the "nurture and admonition of the Lord." Our spouses need much more from us than paychecks.

The Lord and the work of His kingdom often get robbed as a result of debt, as well. The Lord tells us to give to Him as we have been prospered. Debt does not necessarily prevent this, but often causes confusion about what constitutes our "prosperity." Many folks erroneously conclude their prosperity is what they have after all the bills are paid—and this is little or nothing. The Lord, then, gets the leftovers.

If the Lord is not robbed of monetary offerings for His work, He often is robbed of time needed to spread the gospel to the lost. Helping support a gospel preacher is not a substitute for our own involvement in this kingdom work.

Worry is an awful affliction. It also suggests a lack of trust in God. Jesus told us not to worry about what we will eat, drink, or wear (Matthew 6:25-34). For honest people, debt can be a major cause of worry, stress, anger, resentment, and sins accompanying them. Most of modern debt is for things far beyond the basic necessities of life the Lord promises to provide each of us.

### The Bottom Line: Debt And Sin Have A Lot In Common

Debt and sin have much in common. Both advertise greater advantages and happiness than they can deliver. Both seemingly address perceived needs in the short term, but ignore consequences in the long-term. Each is often (sin always) rooted in selfishness instead of great interest in the needs of others. Both usually take us much farther than we had planned to go.

We must remember real Christians seek to imitate God. He is characterized by His love and truthfulness. He never makes a promise He does not keep. It is unimaginable He would harm one of us by defrauding us. It must be our goal to be as much like Him as possible.

Most debt problems stem from undisciplined desires, a lack of patience, and a misguided expectation of happiness being found in what we possess. Jesus warned about this, "Take heed and beware of covetousness, for one's life does not consist in the abundance of the things he possesses" (Luke 12:15).

Finally, in every case where debt and its repayment are considered, let us remember the biblical principle of loving our neighbor as ourselves. Jesus summed up an ethic we should apply in all circumstances. He said, "And just as you want men to do to you, you also do to them likewise" (Luke 6:31). Apply this principle before you make a decision to go into debt. And, if you decide debt is prudent, be sure to apply it as you repay your debt.

## ➢ Questions ◄

1. How would financial or debt pressures create stresses in a marriage great enough a couple would seek a divorce? _____
_____
_____
_____

2. The IRS says average Americans spend 10 times more in interest on their debts than on charitable donations. If this is as true of typical Christians as it is of average Americans, what are the spiritual implications? _____
_____
_____
_____

3. After reading Proverbs 22:7, what does the phrase "the borrower is servant to the lender" mean? _____
_____
_____
_____

4. Define your understanding of "stewardship." Find at least three Bible passages teaching about this subject. _____
_____
_____
_____
_____

5. Do some research concerning various avenues of legally filing bankruptcy. Are any of these acceptable actions for a Christian? Explain why or why not. _____
_____
_____
_____
_____
_____

6. How can one determine the dividing line between what may be prudent borrowing and debt created from greed, impatience, lack of faith in God's provision or a combination of selfishness and lack of self-discipline? _____
_____
_____
_____
_____

7. What are some pros and cons of churches going into debt? _____
_____
_____
_____

# BANKRUPTCY

More than 2,000,000 personal and business bankruptcies were filed in the United States in 2005. This number plummeted the following year because the U.S. Congress passed newer and stricter bankruptcy laws. The number of bankruptcies is on the rise once again.

Once considered a shameful last resort, bankruptcy in the United States has become a socially and legally acceptable method of resolving serious financial problems.

Can a Christian file bankruptcy and still be righteous? While we might seek a simple yes or no answer, God's perspective in Scripture requires us to understand a number of principles and then apply them to the specific case. This is not dodging the question but simply acknowledging the answer lies in the circumstances and details. Neither is this an effort to suggest situation ethics.

Righteousness, under both the Law of Moses and the newer Covenant of Christ, demands God's people be honest, keep their word, and not steal. Psalm 37:21 says, "The wicked borrows and does not repay, but the righteous shows mercy and gives."

When a person uses a credit card, signs a mortgage or other loan papers, or otherwise agrees to pay another person or company, he or she is under a moral obligation to repay the debt. To do otherwise is shameful and dishonorable.

We realize occasions such as natural disasters, sickness, or even death make fulfilling such obligations nearly impossible without help. Yet, to walk away from one's debts to find relief merely transfers the burden to someone else—the creditor. Jesus' injunction to treat others as you would want to be treated, often called the "golden rule," demonstrates the moral pitfall in such an approach (Matthew 7:12; Luke 6:31).

How do we find the answer to this dilemma?

> "The **wicked** borrows and **does not repay**, but the **righteous** shows mercy and **gives**" (Psalms 37:21).

As suggested in the previous lesson on debt, part of the answer is to avoid situations poten-tially leaving you unable to pay what you owe. Just as one can plan on avoiding fornication by avoiding situations and places conducive to such, so one can immensely reduce the likelihood of being unable to pay debts by avoiding or limiting debt secured by some tangible asset.

Christians need to think seriously about the potential impact on their reputations and example. Our lives are more about drawing others to Christ than simply securing a comfortable earthly existence.

Before we proceed further, let us explore what we mean by bankruptcy or filing for bankruptcy.

### What Is Bankruptcy?

Fundamentally, bankruptcy is being in a financial situation where one is unable to pay their debts or obligations. Legally speaking, under federal law, there is a process by which a person or business declares or is declared unable to pay what is owed. The court then determines what will be done.

In trying to ascertain a biblically and morally acceptable behavior, it is important to know not every bankruptcy proceeding has the same process or outcome. For the purposes of this study, there are three types of bankruptcy procedures worth our attention.
- One is called liquidation. Liquidation is known in legal circles as a Chapter 7 proceeding. The debtor's assets (if there are any) are sold, and the money garnered distributed to credi-tors. The remainder of the debt is legally erased. Certain assets, which can include a house, car, and other things, are excluded from the liquidation. Some income sources, like Social Security, cannot be taken to pay the debts.
- Another is known as reorganization. Typically known as Chapter 11 bankruptcy, this approach allows a business to reorganize and continue to operate. Debt may be restructured, new loans obtained, and others reduced, so the business can continue to operate, make money, and eventually pay at least part of what is owed.
- The third is a repayment plan. Known as Chapter 13, this part of the law allows an individual or couple to work out a plan with creditors to repay what is owed. This may involve getting creditors to approve a longer period to pay and thus lower monthly payments. Creditors may voluntarily forgive a portion of the debt to make payment of the remainder feasible. Other terms may be changed by negotiation and then joint agreement.

Let us carefully observe the differences in these "chapters." Some forms of bankruptcy legally allow a person to walk away from paying what they once promised to pay. Other forms of bankruptcy are designed to make it possible for the debtor to fulfill his promise to pay.

As we seek to answer the moral questions about bankruptcy, we must determine what pro-ceeding we are discussing. Not everyone who files for bankruptcy is being dishonest or trying to avoid paying what they owe.

Someone may ask, "Is filing for bankruptcy sinful?" A simple "yes" or "no" answer is not re-sponsible. We must apply all the appropriate biblical principles of moral and ethical behavior to the situation.

## Does The Bible Have A Model For Bankruptcy?

Some have argued the Old Testament's sabbatical year debt cancellation provisions are a precedent and model for the modern concept of bankruptcy (forced debt forgiveness).

The regulation is found in Deuteronomy 15. The first three verses read: "At the end of every seven years you shall grant a release of debts. And this is the form of the release: Every creditor who has lent anything to his neighbor shall release it; he shall not require it of his neighbor or his brother, because it is called the Lord's release. Of a foreigner you may require it; but you shall give up your claim to what is owed by your brother."

Some read this and suggest in Israel every family had a chance to "start over" at least once in a life-time. Others point out it is not clear this legislation wiped out debts permanently. John C. Maxwell points out, "Israelites were not to be pressed to pay their debts during this year. The phrase 'at the end' (v. 1) is included because money debts were not paid until the crops were gathered or the former had been paid. Then he could pay his debts. However, the seventh year was different. There is much debate over whether a debt was to be terminated permanently or suspended for one year, meaning the repayment could not be demanded during the course of the seventh year. The latter alternative seems probable. At the end of seven years all debts that had been contracted were again extended for another year. The total debts were forgiven in the year of Jubilee (every 50th year)" (Maxwell, 1987).

What is obvious is the context of these debt suspensions was radically different from contemporary bankruptcy issues. The challenge for Christians is to learn appropriate lessons from this regulation without trying to force the legislation into a totally different situation.

Also observe:
- What was in view were not commercial loans for business or profit but charitable loans brethren made to the poor among them.
- Such loans were to be made without interest (Exodus 22:25).
- The seventh year debt suspension also must be viewed in the overall context of the sabbatical years. The Israelites were to work their land for six years. In the seventh year, they were not to plant or harvest. The land was to rest. The poor could not plant crops, so demanding repayment in the year God commanded them not to plant crops would have been totally unreasonable and unloving.
- The rule did not apply to non-Israelites ("foreigners) since they were not bound by the rules of the sabbatical year. This was not

**Not** everyone who **files** for bankruptcy is being **dishonest** or trying to **avoid paying** what they owe.

an expression of hatred toward foreigners, just recognition there was no reason for them not to repay their debts during this year.
- The concept of the Sabbath involved "rest." The legislation demanded the poor not be denied the blessings of the year of rest. For a deeper treatment of this issue, see Keil and Delitzsch, Deuteronomy, p. 369ff and Pulpit Commentary, Deuteronomy, p. 253ff.

Today, Christians have no command to keep Sabbath days or years. We can learn a great deal from the Old Testament legislation about how we should treat our brethren and the poor, but to attempt to find in the sabbatical year or Jubilee year legislation a foundation to walk away from legally incurred personal and commercial debts is to ignore the religious and cultural context of the Law of Moses.

### Like Divorce, Bankruptcy Not The Panacea Some Think

TV and radio money management counselor Dave Ramsey says this:

> Bankruptcy is not something I recommend any more than I would recommend divorce. Are there times when good people see no way out and file bankruptcy? Yes, but I will still talk you out of bankruptcy if given the opportunity. Few people who go through bankruptcy would report it is a painless wiping-clean of the slate, after which you merrily trot off into your future to start fresh.

> Don't let anyone fool you. I have been through bankruptcy and have worked with bankruptcy for decades, and it is not a place you want to visit. Bankruptcy is listed in the top 5 life-altering negative events that we can go through, along with divorce, severe illness, disability, and loss of a loved one. I would never say that bankruptcy is as bad as losing a loved one, but it is life-altering and leaves deep wounds both to the psyche and the credit report.

> Chapter 7 bankruptcy, which is total bankruptcy, stays on your credit report for 10 years. Chapter 13, more like a payment plan, stays on your credit report for 7 years. Bankruptcy, however, is for life. Loan applications and many job applications ask if you have ever filed for bankruptcy. Ever. If you lie to get a loan because your bankruptcy is very old, technically you have committed criminal fraud (Ramsey, 2009).

Just as **one** can plan on **avoiding fornication** ... **one** can immensely **reduce** the likelihood of being **unable** to **pay** debts...

**Cited**

Maxwell, J.C. (1987). *Deuteronomy, the communicator's commentary.* Waco, Tx: Word Books Publisher.

Ramsey, D. (2009, August 3). *The truth about bankruptcy.* Retrieved from http://www.foundationssu.com/articles/article/contentname/foundations-the-truth-about-bankruptcy.

## ➤ Questions ◄

1. What is a good definition of bankruptcy? _____
   _____
   _____

2. List some moral principles taught in the Bible which suggest it is sinful to walk away and not pay one's debt. _____
   _____
   _____
   _____

3. What steps can a Christian take to avoid the possibility or probability of bankruptcy? _____
   _____
   _____
   _____

4. What are the three most common forms of bankruptcy filings? _____
   _____
   _____
   _____
   _____

5. Are there any Bible passages which would authorize a Christian to find a legal means for not paying what he promised to pay? If so, be prepared to demonstrate your answer.
   _____
   _____
   _____
   _____

6. Besides the economic impacts of bankruptcy on an individaul, in what other ways can bankruptcy affect an individual's life and their relationships. _____
   _____
   _____
   _____
   _____
   _____

# GIVING: SHARING & WISELY USING GOD'S GIFTS

Giving involves handing over to someone else our time, money or other possessions without the expectation of receiving something in exchange or being paid back. Giving, of course, involves gifts. Such giving involves parting with something solely for the benefit of another person.

Thus, by the definition of giving, we see it is an act of selflessness. True giving is an act of love. It is an act done out of sincere interest in the well-being of another person. Giving should not be done with the expectation of getting something in return.

The biblical concept of giving involves much more than merely giving a donation. The concept of a donation implies we are the owners of our possessions and solely out of the generosity of our hearts are giving some to others.

God's Word certainly urges generosity or liberality in giving, but it also teaches the principle of stewardship, the idea our possessions belong to God. A steward handles the possessions of the owner, according to the owner's directions.

Stewardship is a concept rooted in fact and implemented by an attitude. The book of Genesis records God made the world and everything in it, including man. He instructed man to have "dominion" over the creation (Genesis 1:28).

Stewardship sometimes is wrongly reduced to a mere cliché for fundraising. When viewed scripturally, it primarily describes and defines our relationship with God. If giving is the nature of the Father, it should be the nature of the children of God. If God put gifts into our hands to use for His purposes, how we give or do not give reflects on our relationship with Him (obedient or disobedient, faithful or unfaithful).

> If **giving** is the nature of the **Father**, it should be the nature of the **children** of God.

## Giving Gifts Is A Part Of The Nature Of God

God is love, says John (1 John 4:8, 16). How did God demonstrate His love for humankind? Again, John tells us, "For God so loved the world that He gave His only begotten Son, that whoever believes in Him should not perish but have everlasting life" (John 3:16). How are we to demonstrate love? John says, "But whoever has this world's goods, and sees his brother in need, and shuts up his heart from him, how does the love of God abide in him?" (1 John 3:17).

God's gift of His Son guarantees He will give us other things we need. This was the Apostle Paul's point in Romans 8:32, where he wrote, "He who did not spare His own Son, but delivered Him up for us all, how shall He not with Him also freely give us all things?"

Jesus affirmed the giving nature of God. He said, "So I say to you, ask, and it will be given to you; seek, and you will find; knock, and it will be opened to you. For everyone who asks receives, and he who seeks finds, and to him who knocks it will be opened. If a son asks for bread from any father among you, will he give him a stone? Or if he asks for a fish, will he give him a serpent instead of a fish? Or if he asks for an egg, will he offer him a scorpion? If you then, being evil, know how to give good gifts to your children, how much more will your heavenly Father give the Holy Spirit to those who ask Him!" (Luke 11:9-13).

The very concept and origin of both giving and gifts is divine. James 1:17 declares, "Every good gift and every perfect gift is from above, and comes down from the Father of lights, with whom there is no variation or shadow of turning."

Grace and mercy, two other attributes of God, are reflected in His giving nature. Grace involves kindness and goodwill reflected in the bestowal of unearned or unmerited favor. God's is gracious (1 Peter 2:3) and is most clearly seen in the salvation offered those who will have faith in God's Son, given as a sacrifice for sin.

Mercy is an outward manifestation of pity toward those in need. Mercy is shown by grace—or the giving of gifts to alleviate suffering or need. Again, mercy is part of the character of God. In fact, He is the "father of mercies" (Ephesians 2:4-10; 2 Corinthians 1:3).

## Giving Nature Opposite Of Greedy, Uncaring, Materialistic Character

Love and giving are intertwined. All the opposites of love—including hate and selfishness—are exhibited by the greedy, materialistic, uncaring character of the person who seeks to keep all his possessions for himself.

Perhaps no greater contrast is seen than in the last hours of Jesus' life. He was making preparation to give the ultimate gift, His life. Simultaneously, Judas was preparing to betray the Lord for 30 pieces of silver, having already stolen from the disciple's treasury (Matthew 26:39, 42; 26:14-16; John 12:6, 13:29).

The giving Christians are called upon to undertake does not involve just money. The Apostle Paul wrote, "I beseech you therefore, brethren, by the mercies of God, that you present your bodies a living sacrifice, holy, acceptable to God, which is your reasonable service" (Romans 12:1).

Having observed our whole life is sought as a living sacrifice, let us remember time and money are measures of and part of our life. Thus, our sacrifice will include gifts of both time and money. Paul noted an illustration of this in the action of the Macedonian Christians who "first gave themselves to the Lord" and then a sacrificial monetary gift for the needy saints in Jerusalem (2 Corinthians 8:1-5).

### One Function Of Work Is To Have Something To Give

In the highly materialistic world in which we live, it often is forgotten even among those with a strong "work ethic" one of the reasons God commended and commanded work is so we will have assets to share with others. The Apostle Paul made this very clear. "Let him who stole steal no longer, but rather let him labor, working with his hands what is good, that he may have something to give him who has need" (Ephesians 4:28).

It is commendable when Christians work to provide for their own (1 Peter 5:8). Likewise, it is God's will if a man will not work he should not eat (2 Thessalonians 3:6-12). We must not forget the third purpose of work, to have enough beyond meeting our own needs and those of our extended family to give aid to others.

### Old Testament Tithing Model

While New Testament Christians are not bound to the specific rule of tithing (a 10 percent offering) because it was part of the old covenant nailed to the cross (Colossians 2:14), the Old Testament giving system serves as a foundational model for how Christians should both view and use their material possessions. Like other elements of the old law, including Sabbath keeping, food and drink restrictions, and various festivals, tithing was a "shadow" of the reality to be developed in Christ's kingdom. There remains much for Christians to learn from this shadow regarding giving.

The very **concept** of both **giving** and **gifts** is **divine**.

First, the tithing system taught God's people giving is to be systematic or habitual, as well as proportional and tied to individual ability. We see a similar concept in 1 Corinthians 16:1-2, in the New Testament, where it speaks of a regular day for giving and basing our giving on our prosperity.

We learn in Deuteronomy 14:23 tithing was intended to teach Israel to "fear the Lord your God always." It trained the people to put God first in their lives. The tithes were not like a tip, but represented a significant economic expression of gratitude to God, Who gave them all they had. It required one to count his blessings and then calculate what should be given.

In our day the idea of giving 10 percent of one's income is viewed as either an oppressively heavy demand, as evidence of supreme generosity, or both. The Jews were actually giving much more than a simple 10 percent of their possessions. It probably was

...trying to merely create a program for **what I "owe"** is counterproductive, since it **may strip** the gift of its **love** component. On the other hand, we are sometimes **thoughtless** about the **true "basis"** for calculating what is **reasonably expected** of us.

closer to 23 percent, since they were under obligation to give three different tithes.

- One tithe was given to support the priests and Levites—Leviticus 27:30-34.
- Another tenth of what remained was the festival tithe, to be taken to Jerusalem—Deuteronomy 12:5-7, 14:22-27.
- Lastly, there was a charity tithe, given during the third year for the Levites, strangers, orphans and widows—Deuteronomy 26:12, 14:28-29.

While the texts already noted demonstrate tithing was a part of the Law of Moses, it is worthwhile to note the practice of tithing preceded this law. The first reference is found in Genesis 14:18-20 where Abraham, father of the Jewish nation, gave a tithe to Melchizedek, a priest of God and king of Salem. We also observe in Genesis 28:22 Jacob promised to give God a tithe.

Both of these passages are useful in helping us determine what we are to base our giving upon. Both Abraham and Jacob gave a tithe of "all" they had. In the New Testament, we are told to give as we are "prospered." Abraham and Jacob's examples help us understand of what our prosperity consists. (See also Leviticus 27:32; Deuteronomy 14:23).

It also is worth noting, as with many other Old Testament patterns, tithing is not the fulfillment of God's desire for our giving, but merely an elementary, educational pattern. As one writer has suggested, "Tithing isn't the finish line of giving; it's the starting blocks."

Sadly, most Christians may be stuck on the starting blocks or not even "set" that far. The Lord's desire for us is not a mere mechanical gift of duty, but an imbibing of His love of gift giving.

### How Do We Determine Our Prosperity?

One of the great challenges to generous or liberal giving is an accurate assessment of our prosperity. Some falsely imagine prosperity to be what is left after all our bills are paid. Considering in 2006 and 2007 Americans as a whole had a negative savings rate, such an approach leaves nothing to be given to God or others in many instances.

Even if there is something left, this approach simply gives God or God's purposes the "leftovers." This hardly imitates the pattern of God's own giving nature.

It is not within the scope of this author's knowledge or wisdom to create an absolute standard for every individual's calculation of prosperity. Given the Old Testament worthies based their tithe on "all" they possessed, can we calculate our prosperity only on our "take home" pay, after insurances, taxes, retirement investments, and the like are subtracted? Do we logically exclude investment income, including interest, dividends, capital gains, and other various profits?

Again, trying to merely create a program for what I "owe" is counterproductive, since it may strip the gift of its love component. On the other hand, we are sometimes thoughtless about the true "basis" for calculating what is reasonably expected of us.

### Use Of Our Money Is A Barometer Of Spirituality

Many of us are familiar with the Apostle Paul's assertion "the love of money is the root of all evil" (1 Tim. 6:10). Have we considered the way we use our money is a barometer of our spirituality? Observe what the same apostle writes in Galatians 6:6-10. In particular, he writes in verses 7-8, "Do not be deceived, God is not mocked; for whatever a man sows, that he will also reap. For he who sows to his flesh will of the flesh reap corruption, but he who sows to the Spirit will of the Spirit reap everlasting life."

If we "sow to the flesh," we keep most of our earthly resources for the purpose of making our physical life more comfortable and pleasurable. If we "sow to the Spirit," we will be giving people, seeking to fulfill God's purposes. This giving will go beyond a mere church contribution, though it is included, because evangelizing the world, edifying the saints and helping needy saints requires financial support. This latter sowing will include additional gifts reflecting the love of God in our lives. Notice in the text, the context is giving of financial resources.

Paul connects investment and reward in this passage. A farmer is foolhardy who skimps on seed to save money during planting season. He only hurts only himself at harvest time. The apostle demonstrates in the spiritual realm the same is true. If we try to "save money" during our physical life by being selfish and greedy, we only hurt ourselves at the spiritual harvest time which will occur at the Lord's return and judgment.

Paul sounds a bit like an investment counselor. Those who handle stock market and mutual fund investments always advise to think "long term" and not get overly excited about the ups and downs of the market. Likewise, Paul urges us not to "grow weary" in doing good, because in the proper season, we will reap our reward. Sometimes Christians begin to grow weary in their giving because they do not see an immediate return. We are wise to avoid such short term views.

### Giving Blesses The Giver

The Apostle Paul quotes words of Jesus not found in the gospels. The Lord said, "It is more blessed to give than to receive" (Acts 20:35). This is counterintuitive to the worldly minded, because selfishness never imagines blessing in anything but receiving.

We can best see the truth of Jesus' words when we look at the miser. He is a greedy person who cannot enjoy what he has, though he hoards. The miser is miserable. His possessions do not bless him.

On the other hand, the more giving or sharing we are, the more we find life to be satisfying and happy. Doing good and helping others makes the person giving the help feel good himself. This is true mentally, spiritually, and even physiologically.

## Various New Testament Instructions On Giving For Work Of The Kingdom

Having taken a general look at the concept and origins of giving, and having observed some lessons to be learned from Old Testament giving regulations, it now is imperative that we explore what New Testament Christians are instructed about giving. We learn in the New Testament that our giving is to be:

### Voluntary

While the New Testament teaches contributing to the work of the kingdom is a command (1 Cor. 16:1-2), it is to be done voluntarily to be pleasing to the Lord. The Apostle Paul spoke of such giving being done with a "willing mind" (2 Cor. 8:12) and not as "a grudging obligation" or done "grudgingly or of necessity" (2 Cor. 9:5, 7). This is not an example of scriptures conflicting. God's demand is we be givers like Him. What sort of "gift" is given unwillingly?

### Regular, Planned, And Deliberate

In his directions to the Corinthian church cited above, the Apostle Paul said the Christians should give on the first day of the week (the day of worship). We can logically and necessarily conclude since there is a first day in every week, worship and giving should be on a regular weekly basis. The Israelites understood this principle regarding keeping the Sabbath.

Paul directed Christians' giving be planned, when he wrote, "let each one of you lay something aside, storing up as he may prosper". This requires one to assess his prosperity and then deliberate regarding what proportion should be given to further the work of the church. The apostle also spoke of giving as we "purpose" or decide in our hearts (2 Cor. 9:7).

This would seem to necessitate more than just seeing what's left in one's wallet on the Lord's Day.

### Proportional

God does not expect us to give what we do not possess (2 Cor. 8:12). The phrase already alluded to—"storing up as he may prosper"—delineates God's desire we give according to our ability. If one Christian is prospered or earns appreciably more than another, his giving ought also to be appreciably more and vice versa.

### Sacrificial

While our giving should be proportional to our prosperity, sacrificial giving is particularly pleasing to the Lord. In one sense, any giving is sacrificial because we sacrifice or give up what those funds could have bought for our personal wants. The Macedonian Christians were held up as an example to the Corinthian church because "in a great trial of affliction the abundance of their joy and their deep poverty abounded in the riches of their liberality." Paul said, "For I bear witness that according to their ability, yes, and beyond their ability, they were freely willing, imploring us with much urgency that we would receive the gift and the fellowship of the ministering to the saints. And not only as we had hoped, but they first gave themselves to the Lord, and then to us by the will of God" (2 Cor. 8:2-5).

## Generous

Sacrificial giving has much in common with generosity. Several times in his exhortation to the church at Corinth in the second letter to them, Paul mentioned the need for giving to be generous, bountiful, and with liberality. He stated it also in the negative, urging they not give sparingly (9:5-14). Generosity implies both a willingness to give and liberality. It implies nobility.

## Cheerful

God loves the cheerful giver (2 Cor. 9:7). This verse also speaks of giving as we purpose or plan in our hearts. Giving is to be something we think about and want to do because we love God, His kingdom, His people, and those still lost in sin. The opposite is giving grudgingly, that is, with reluctance because we really do not want to do so.

You can see God's point. What sort of "gift" is pried from the giver's hands?

## Quiet

Jesus taught this aspect of giving in His great Sermon on the Mount. In the first four verses of Matthew 6, Jesus said we should not do our charitable deeds to be seen of men, to get their recognition. He directed we do such giving or helps secretly or quietly. He directed we not give even too much inward, personal thought to our good deed, saying "do not let your left hand know what your right hand is doing." The idea is simply to do good for the sake of doing good, and not be concerned about attention, recognition, or even personally patting ourselves on the back. Let God give us our ultimate reward.

## As Part Of Our Worship

A number of lessons can be learned from the animal and meal sacrifices of the Old Testament. Certainly, the shedding of blood pointed forward to God's plan to give the life of His Son for the sins of the world. We also observe these sacrifices were a central element of worship among the Israelites. Living in an agricultural or pastoral environment, the millions of daily, weekly and annual sacrifices also represented considerable sacrifice economically for the Israelites.

With Jesus' death on the cross, the need and requirement for blood sacrifices ended (Hebrews 10:1-18). Sacrifice was not totally eliminated from New Testament worship. We learn in Hebrews 13:15, "Therefore by Him let us continually offer the sacrifice of praise to God, that is, the fruit of our lips, giving thanks to His name." We give up time and other endeavors to pray to God and sing praises to his name.

The setting aside of the "first" day of the week for worship is a sacrifice, and so are the gifts or contributions we make to the work of the kingdom. We sacrifice or give up the physical goods and services those monies could provide us to further the purposes of God's kingdom. Thus, it is part of our worship and honor of God.

We see the timing of these contributions as being concurrent with the day of worship authorized in the New Testament, when other acts of worship, like the Lord's Supper, teaching, singing and prayer, were conducted (1 Cor. 16:1-2; Acts 20:7).

### Robbing God: Crimes involving improper giving and use of Lord's money

The prophet Malachi rebuked God's people for their failures to give as they had been instructed. He called the sin robbery. "Will a man rob God? Yet you have robbed Me! But you say, 'In what way have we robbed You?' In tithes and offerings" (Malachi 3:8).

The Old Testament patterns established that God expects us to use a certain proportion of our prosperity to accomplish His purposes, not merely to serve our own wants. The New Testament does not define a percentage God expects, but speaks in terms of cheerful, generous, proportional giving. To keep the portion belonging to God's purposes remains equivalent to stealing or robbery.

Again, the case of Ananias and Sapphira in Acts 5 is illustrative of God's attitude toward such thievery.

Another way God may be robbed is by using the gifts contributed for the work of the kingdom for secular purposes and for things not authorized as the work of the church. A careful study of the New Testament will establish three general areas of work the church is authorized to accomplish:
- Evangelism (teaching the gospel)
- Edification (building up the body of Christ)
- Limited benevolence (helping needy saints)

Whenever unauthorized additional endeavors are undertaken and funded, time and money is diverted from the God-given mission of the church. Considering Christians are stewards of this money, it is the equivalent of embezzlement or misappropriation of funds to use them for purposes not authorized by the Lord.

### Christian Gift-giving To Extend Beyond Church Contributions

While the uses of the church treasury are delineated and limited in scripture, it is important to realize God's expectations for Christian giving extend beyond Lord's Day church contributions and their purposes.

The story of the Good Samaritan (Luke 10) illustrates God's expectation of helping our neighbors, including those who may not be Christians. The exhortation in Ephesians 4:28 is to work or labor so we have something to give to those who are in need. The teaching does not specify merely giving to needy saints here.

While there is no authority to take money from the church treasury to assist needy unbelievers, the obligation still exists for Christians to otherwise assist their needy, non-Christian neighbors.

### ➢ Questions ◄

1. Why is the concept of stewardship involved in giving? _____
_____
_____
_____
_____

2. Why is the origin of giving and gifts divine? _____
_____
_____
_____

3. Explain how the example of giving by the Macedonians (2 Cor. 8:1-5) is contrary to the spirit of materialism. _____
_____
_____
_____

4. Is the Old Testament tithing a good model for Christians today to determine how much should be given? _____
_____
_____
_____
_____

5. Why are the ways one spends their money a good barometer for determing what to give?
_____
_____
_____
_____

6. Why is it "more blessed to give than receive" (Acts 20:35)? _____
_____
_____
_____
_____
_____

7. List four key characteristics concernging giving as identified by the New Testament. __
_____
_____
_____
_____
_____

8. At what point does one become guilty of robbing God? _____
_____
_____
_____
_____
_____

# GIVING: ILLUSTRATED

Jesus spoke a great deal about money and possessions during His time on earth. He spoke often about giving.

### Gifts No Substitute For Other Duties, Righteousness

Much of the Lord's earliest teaching on giving is found in His Sermon on the Mount (Matthew 5-7). He first points out making a religious gift (church contribution) is not inherently righteous when a person hates his brother or has acted unrighteously toward him. Jesus instructed, "Therefore if you bring your gift to the altar, and there remember that your brother has something against you, leave your gift there before the altar, and go your way. First be reconciled to your brother, and then come and offer your gift" (Matthew 5:23-24).

Later, in one of His many scathing denunciations of Pharisaical hypocrisy, He made the same general point in another manner. He said, "But woe to you Pharisees! For you tithe mint and rue and all manner of herbs, and pass by justice and the love of God. These you ought to have done, without leaving the others undone" (Luke 11:42). Jesus made clear being scrupulous about tithing or making offerings to the Lord is not a substitute for adhering to the "weightier matters of the law" (Matthew 23:23).

**Giving** is fundamentally an **expression** of a righteous **heart**.

### Proper Purpose In Giving Essential

Continuing in the Sermon on the Mount, Jesus demonstrated true righteousness in religious duties and opportunities requires having the proper motivation and purpose. He demonstrated His point in three examples, but the first involved "charitable deeds" or "almsgiving" (Matthew 6:1-4).

Jesus said, "Take heed that you do not do your charitable deeds before men, to be seen by them. Otherwise you have no reward from your Father in heaven. Therefore, when you do a charitable deed, do not sound a trumpet before you as the hypocrites do in the synagogues and in the streets, that they may have glory from men. Assuredly, I say to you, they have their reward."

Remember what we learned in the last lesson about giving.  It is something done without expectation of exchange or returning benefit. It is to be based on love, mercy, and gracious-ness. If a person gives their gift for the purpose of being commended by men, the act loses its essential nature as a gift.

Jesus indicates God will not ultimately reward such fake giving. Such "givers" receive on earth what they bargained for, the adulation of their fellow men.

The Lord even shows we should not even be too focused on the fact we have done something noteworthy. In other words, do not be too ready to pat your on the back. Just do the good deed because it is good. Jesus words this in a particularly interesting way. "But when you do a charitable deed, do not let your left hand know what your right hand is doing"  (Matt. 6:3).

The Lord illustrates the error of giving to be seen of men or to get a pat on the back in the story of the Pharisee and the tax collector in Luke 18:9-14. The Pharisee in the story was quite typical of both the sect he was a part of and the error Jesus wanted to expose. First, the Pharisee, who trusted he was righteous, boldly and publicly bragged of his goodness so others could hear him. One of his exalted claims was he gave "tithes of all I possess." Jesus contrasted him to the tax collector who would not even look up, but begged for mercy as a sinner.

Giving is fundamentally an expression of a righteous heart. Jesus illustrates this in His story of the widow and her two mites in Luke 21:1-4 (also Mark 12:41-42). Jesus declared her tiny gift greater than the gifts of those who gave large amounts from their great prosperity. Hers represented all she possessed. Such a modest gift likely would seem inconsequential to a human observer unable to see her heart. She must have had a great love and commitment to give all she had.

It may be worth noting Jesus was neither criticizing the larger amounts given, nor directing all men give everything they possess. He certainly was not encouraging men to be stingy in giving. Actually, quite the opposite is the necessary inference.

### Parable Of The Good Samaritan

In His parable of the Good Samaritan (Luke 10:25-37), Jesus illustrated the relationship between our giving or charitable actions and fulfilling the law or pleasing God. A lawyer stood up to test the Lord and asked what he needed to do to inherit eternal life. Jesus asked the lawyer what the law taught. The scribe accurately outlined the two main thrusts of the law, to love God totally and to love your neighbor as yourself. Jesus confirmed his answer as correct. The Lord gave a similar answer Himself as recorded in Matthew 22:34-40 and Mark 12:28-31.

His inquisitor then asks, "and who is my brother?" This prompts the story of the man robbed, beaten, and left for dead on the road between Jerusalem and Jericho. A priest and a Levite both pass by and give no aid. Then a Samaritan, despised by the Jews, sees the man, has compassion, gives him medical aid, and takes him to an inn, paying for his continued care.

Jesus asked which of the three men acted as a "neighbor" to the wounded man. His point again digs to the heart of the matter. The gifts of time, aid, and money came as a result of the Samaritan's compassion. Within his compassion was love and gracious mercy toward his fellow man.

Thus, the student of Jesus' lesson learns the real merit is not so much in the gift, but the attitude and righteous disposition prompting it.

The priest and the Levite likely gave tithes. Yet, they lacked the divine characteristics making it honorable.

### The Widow's Two Mites

One day Jesus sat at the temple opposite the treasury watching as people put their money in the collection. Rich people put in significant amounts. A poor widow came along and threw in two mites. Because it was all she had, Jesus said she had given more than all the others (Mark 12:41-44; Luke 21:1-4).

Jesus did not call attention to this poor woman to justify the giving of a pittance when one can do much better. Quite the opposite, He demonstrated proportionally this woman gave the most because she gave 100 percent of what she possessed. While the others gave vastly greater amounts, proportionally they gave much less.

For the widow, her gift was a major sacrifice and undoubtedly rooted in both love of God and faith in Him. The widow gave what was in her heart. Others gave what was in their hands.

> The **widow gave** what was in her **heart**. **Others gave** what was in their **hands**.

### New Testament Examples

It is one thing to look at the principles of giving enumerated in Scripture. It is more powerful thing to look at those principles brought to life. Let us examine how the Lord's church in its first generation gave of their earthly possessions. Interestingly, the first two "church problems" recorded in Scripture involved giving.

### Giving Directly Tied To Receipt Of God's Gift Of Salvation

The earliest Christians in Jerusalem evidenced their appreciation for God's gift by becoming givers themselves. We read in Acts 2:44-45, "Now all who believed were together, and had all things in common, and sold their possessions and goods, and divided them among all, as anyone had need."

The focus of these first converts to the Christian faith was spiritual. They were full of love and concern for one another. Selfishness appeared, at least temporarily, to have disappeared.

Luke records "the multitude of those who believed were of one heart and one soul; neither did anyone say that any of the things

"for **all** who were possessors of lands or houses **sold** them, and **brought** the proceeds of the things that were sold and **laid** them at the apostles' feet; and they **distributed** to each as anyone had **need**" (Acts 4:34-35).

he possessed was his own, but they had all things in common (Acts 4:32).

As a result, no one among those early disciples originally lacked "for all who were possessors of lands or houses sold them, and brought the proceeds of the things that were sold and laid them at the apostles' feet; and they distributed to each as anyone had need" (Acts 4:34-35).

One man, who later became the Apostle Paul's first preaching companion, is particularly singled out as an example of this type of generosity. He was Barnabas. He sold land and brought it to the apostles for use (Acts 4:36-37).

It often has been debated whether this example of the earliest church serves as a model we should replicate today. There seems no doubt their example of selflessness, spirituality, and love for one another is deserving of imitation. The situation itself may be unique and not be a crisis the present day church will face. So, just as the Lord's directive to the rich young ruler to sell all he had and give to the poor may not apply to us (if we are not trusting in our earthly wealth), this approach in the early church may not find its parallel today.

Even with this caveat, there are great lessons to be learned from their example.

### Ananias And Sapphira—Acts 5:1-11

After being made aware of the loving kindness of Barnabas and the other saints, we are brought face to face with new Christians of a different spiritual temperament. The very first sin dealt with by the new Jerusalem church involved deception and hypocrisy relating to a gift.

A husband and wife, Ananias and Sapphira, did similarly to Barnabas and sold a piece of real estate. They brought a part of the sale proceeds and laid them at the apostles' feet, apparently leaving the impression they had given the whole amount derived from the sale.

Peter made it clear they were not obligated to give the total sale price to the church. Regardless of how much they gave, they did "lie," telling the apostles it was the entire amount fromt the sale.

Both of them were struck dead by God because of their gifting fraud. Fortunately, for those who rob God or deceive their brethren about their giving today, God has not been striking such sinners dead as of late. Imagine if He did. Luke twice records "great fear came upon all those who heard these things" and "upon all the church."

It is worthwhile to recognize while God does not render such immediate judgment today, His judgment of such behavior is just as sure, even if delayed.

### The Grecian Widows—Acts 6:1-7

The second problem in the new Jerusalem church also entailed giving. As the number of disciples grew (they began with 3,000 and quickly grew to 5,000 or more—Acts 2:41; 4:4; 5:14), there were some Greek-speaking widows in the church that were not receiving a share of the "daily distribution."

Cultural differences might have created great problems in the early church, but this was averted when a group of seven men (similar to deacons) were appointed to see the material needs of the congregation were equitably addressed.

It is interesting to observe the generosity of the early saints appears to have had some part in the continued growth of their number. Acts 6:7 says after this problem was addressed, "the word of God spread, and the number of the disciples multiplied greatly."

This was not because people were looking for a free lunch, but because the early saints were imitating the grace of God in their own graciousness toward their brethren. It was faith in action and demonstrably powerful testimony.

In this example, we find authority for one of the three primary missions of the church—caring for needy saints. A special group of seven men were appointed to oversee and handle this distribution of gifts. This is one of the functions deacons today continue to fulfill.

### Dealing with the crisis created by a famine—Acts 11:28-30

While the Jerusalem crisis involving the Grecian widows shows what a local congregation can and should do in dealing with need among its own members, the Judean famine illustrates what a group of congregations can do to relieve needy saints outside their own number.

In Acts 11:28-30, we read of a prophet named Agabus foretelling a famine to come in Judea. He was speaking in Antioch at the time. As a result, "the disciples, each according to his ability, determined to send relief to the brethren dwelling in Judea." They sent the funds to the elders in Judea, with Barnabas and Paul carrying the gift.

A couple of things need to be emphasized here:
- These funds were for assisting needy saints, not Judeans in general. We find no command, example, or even concrete inference churches are to assist non-Christians. Certainly, individual Christians have such obligations, but not the church.
- The money was delivered to the elders of churches in Judea for distribution. The Antioch church did not attempt a direct distribution to individuals. They did not usurp the leadership and oversight of the local elders.

### Needy Saints In Jerusalem

In Paul's letter to the church at Rome, he mentions Christians in Greece (Macedonia and Achaia) had made a contribution for the needy saints in Jerusalem. Paul was going to deliver the funds. Paul said the Gentile saints in Greece saw it appropriate to give this material help, since the Jewish Christians had a role in bringing spiritual blessings to the Gentiles (Rom. 15:25-28).

Our very example of when to give comes in connection with this gift for the needy saints in Jerusalem. In 1 Corinthians 16:1-4 we read: "Now concerning the collection for the saints, as I have given orders to the churches of Galatia, so you must do also: On the first day of the week let each one of you lay something aside, storing up as he may prosper, that there be no collections when I come. And when I come, whomever you approve by your letters I will send to bear your gift to Jerusalem. But if it is fitting that I go also, they will go with me."

In his second letter to the Corinthians, in chapters 8 and 9, Paul tells the Christians in Corinth (Achaia) of the liberality of the Macedonian Christians in giving even in their poverty for the needy in Jerusalem. He is using the example of one group of Christians to encourage another group to do the same.

We learn in these chapters Corinth had committed to helping a year earlier, but had not carried through their plan.

In these chapters we learn:
- Paul spoke of such giving as a "grace."
- He saw giving as a measure or test of love.
- Giving needs to be something a person wants to do, not a compelled thing.
- Gifts should be based on ability, but are especially significant when sacrificial.
- Giving is like seed planting; the one who sows sparingly, reaps sparingly and the one who sows bountifully, reaps bountifully.
- Our generous giving causes men to thank and glorify God.

The Corinthians in Achaia had been slow to send the money they had planned to give. Good intentions had not translated into action when Paul sent brethren to Corinth to encourage them and when he wrote his second letter.

We do not know for sure why these brethren had not kept their commitment. We might be able to make an educated supposition based on part of Paul's response. Many of us have found ourselves desirous of helping others, but fearful we will not have enough left for ourselves.

Paul addressed this concern when he wrote, "And God is able to make all grace abound toward you, that you, always having all sufficiency in all things, may have an abundance for every good work. As it is written: 'He has dispersed abroad, He has given to the poor; His righteousness endures forever.' Now may He who supplies seed to the sower, and bread for food, supply and multiply the seed you have sown and increase the fruits of your righteousness, while you are enriched in everything for all liberality, which causes thanksgiving through us to God" (9:8-11). In other words, we should not forget God gives to us. Thus, He gives us the ability to help others. We need to trust in that fact.

## ➤ Questions ◄

1. Why can one's giving not be a substitute for righteousness? _____
_____
_____
_____
_____

2. What should be the Christians motivation for doing charitable deeds and giving? __

_____
_____
_____
_____

3. What can be learned about one's possessions from the parable of the good Samaritan?

_____
_____
_____
_____

4. Identify the differences between what the widow gave versus what others contributed.

_____
_____
_____
_____
_____

5. What is the likely reason the early church in Jerusalem so freely willing to give of their possesseions? _____

_____
_____
_____
_____

6. Considering the early church, why has God given possessions to us? _____

_____
_____
_____
_____
_____

CPSIA information can be obtained
at www.ICGtesting.com
Printed in the USA
FFHW010815060119
50052215-54853FF